Jeffrey Green has researched the pre-*Windrush* black presence in Britain for decades, assisted by veterans such as Leslie Thompson, and has presented his findings in many articles and books, on radio and television, and at conferences. His articles can be found in the *Oxford Dictionary of National Biography*, the *New Grove Dictionary of Jazz*, the *Oxford Companion to Black British History*, the *Journal of Caribbean History*, *Black Music Research Journal* and *New Community*. He is the author of a biography of the South Carolina-born, London-educated composer Edmund Thornton Jenkins, and of *Black Edwardians: Black People in Britain 1901–1914*. He contributed to Bernth Lindfors, *Africans on Stage* (1999); Samuel Floyd, *Black Music in the Harlem Renaissance* (1993) and Neil Wynn, *Cross the Water Blues: African American Music in Europe* (2007). A guitarist, liking 1920s and 1930s jazz, he worked in Uganda in the late 1960s and has travelled globally as an export manager and for curiosity.

Swing from a Small Island

the story of Leslie Thompson

Swing from a Small Island

the story of Leslie Thompson

Leslie Thompson

with Jeffrey Green

Northway Publications
39 Tytherton Road, London N19 4PZ, UK.
www.northwaybooks.com

Front cover photo of Kingston Harbour, 1909, courtesy of the Royal Commonwealth Society. The publishers acknowledge with thanks the kind permission of copyright holders to reprint the photographs used in this book. Permissions have been sought in all cases where the identity of the copyright holders is known. Where no source is credited, photos are from Leslie Thompson's collection.

Cover design by Adam Yeldham of Raven Design.

First published in 1985 by Rabbit Press Ltd with the title: *Leslie Thompson – an autobiography*.

This edition published 2009.

A CIP record for this book is available from the British Library.

ISBN 978 09557888 2 6

Printed and bound in Great Britain by Cromwell Press Group, Trowbridge, Wiltshire.

'My son, if thou wilt receive my words, and hide my commandments with thee, so that thou incline thine ear unto wisdom, and apply thine heart to understanding. Yea if thou criest after knowledge, and liftest up thy voice for understanding; if thou seekest her as silver and searchest for her, as for hid treasure, then shalt thou understand the fear of the Lord, and find the knowledge of God.'

Proverbs of Solomon the son of David, King of Israel, chapter 2.

CONTENTS

Preface   xi

1.   Jamaica   1

2.   Profession: Musician   26

3.   My Face is my Fortune   57

4.   Bombardier, Cellist   105

5.   Warden   129

6.   Probation and Prison   140

7.   Tony   149

8.   Africa and Jamaica   159

9.   Reflections   170

Notes   177

Further Reading   183

Appendices   185
    A.   'Value and Perspective' 1935
    B.   Opinions
    C.   Blindfold Test

Glossary   193

Index   195

PREFACE

Showbusiness people are famous for the superlatives which they use to describe their friends and often themselves. Leslie Anthony Joseph Thompson was a more modest man, of great charm, whose lucidity reflected a great deal of thought. He did not sprinkle his conversations with names and in the preparation of this book I found myself applying gentle pressure to get details from him.

I first met with Leslie Thompson at the suggestion of John Chilton and produced an article which was published by *Black Perspective in Music* of New York in early 1984, but there was much beyond the focus of that academic journal. As well as his life in music in Jamaica and Britain there were the tales of Alpha Cottage School and the West India Regiment, the Hitler war years, his work with students, his time in the probation service, and his wide range of contacts from Louis Armstrong and Noel Coward to Fats Waller, Louis Drysdale, Vera Manley, Marcus Garvey, the Mills Brothers, and Festo Kivengere in Uganda.

Between January and November 1985 I met with him at his Gower Street, Bloomsbury flat where he told me about his life. I typed up the notes, mailed them to him, and a week or two later would go back to central London where we would discuss those notes. Leslie added details, corrected names, and made suggestions before we continued. The full text was submitted and he made further alterations. The autobiography was first published in December 1985.

He died at the nearby hospital on 20 December 1987. I went, with two veterans of the 1930s, to his funeral at Westminster Chapel. I was surprised to hear that as well as his son Tony there had been a daughter – Leslie did not mention her. This was his story. The names he mentioned had been checked – from

Bedward, a folk-religious leader in 1910s Jamaica, to Dr J. J. Brown, a medical practitioner in east London in the 1930s. I had the pleasure of taking Leslie to meet Dr Brown's son in Norfolk. I did not identify the Barbados-born fellow who was elected to Paddington council in 1946 nor did I press Leslie for more details of his views of Marcus Garvey. His religious beliefs, which from the 1950s were profound, led him to write the chapter 'Reflections'. That was not the result of our regular discussions, but his wish – which, typically, he first raised with church colleagues.

Raymond Skinner, a church friend, wrote his obituary in the *Independent* (5 January 1988) which ended, 'His firm faith, daily Bible readings, calm courtesy and ability to "get alongside" people, allied to worldwide letter-writing, made him in heavy demand until the last.' That was Leslie Thompson, but there was his sense of humour, always gentle, which would have led him to smile at the *Observer*'s obituary (27 December 1987) which stated he was 'one of Britain's greatest black jazz musicians'. This view was one that the slightly longer obituary in *The Times* (2 January 1988) duplicated: 'one of this country's finest jazz musicians' but it also said 'He was seldom ruffled, and had the gift of getting close to those in distress.'

At the funeral I was struck by the dimensions of the coffin. Leslie Thompson was never that small, surely? It was, but he wasn't.

I welcome the reprint of the 1985 book (with valuable corrections from Morten Clausen and Peter W. G. Powell) for I am convinced that Leslie Thompson's story is one of great interest. His life was rich and his contribution was generous.

Jeffrey Green
East Grinstead, West Sussex
June 2009

ACKNOWLEDGEMENTS

The comments, questions, responses, assistance and generosity of the following made the authors' task easier and their contributions are gratefully acknowledged: Jeff Aldam, Amy Barbour-James, Arthur Briggs, Leslie and Moira Brown, John Chilton, Bill Colyer, John Cowley, Eustace Cummings, Rudolph Dunbar, Joe Deniz, Charles Frost, Peter Fryer, Christopher Fyfe, George Green, Ronald Green, Chris Hayes, Manny Henriques, Nigel 'Cod' Hill, Rainer Lotz, Harvey McKenzie, Tony Martin, Paul McGilchrist, National Library of Jamaica, Ian Pegg, Royal Commonwealth Society, Howard Rye, Donald Simpson, Sister Marie Therese, Storyville (Laurie Wright), Shirley Thompson, Dave Wilkins, Brian Willan, Morten Clausen and Peter W. G. Powell.

1

Jamaica

I was born in Kingston, Jamaica, on 17 October 1901, the year Queen Victoria died. I came to London in 1929 and have lived here ever since, although I did return to Jamaica in 1980 to see my sister Maria and to have a look at things. I was born at the Lying-in Hospital in North Street, and named Leslie Anthony Joseph. My parents, Charlotte and Emmanuel Thompson, had five children. My other sisters and brother Vincent died some years ago. My first recollection was as a toddler; certainly I could walk after a fashion. I can remember playing with the other children. As a teeny, weeny, little lad I played all the time, if my memory is correct.

Looking back, in the light of a good few years, I can see that turn-of-the-century Kingston had marked social divisions. The business and trading community had its offices and ware-houses located near the docks, and labourers and their families settled in the area, to be close to work. The Europeans lived up the hill for the most part, and there was a big divide between the races. But Kingston wasn't very large, even if Jamaica was the most populous island in the British West Indies, and there were contacts between the races.

Economic stagnation suggested that opportunities would be found elsewhere, and many Jamaicans went off to America, often via Cuba or Panama. The Canal was being constructed at

Panama and thousands of West Indians worked there. My mother went there, to Panama, in 1911; I don't know what she did, but she came back to see us a couple of times. In Jamaica the stagnation affected everyone, and one reason why the relationship between the races was affable and smooth was because the economic stability of Jamaicans depended completely on the whites, and this was realised. They needed the workers, and the workers needed the money.

My father went out to work every day but really and truly I cannot say what he did, either. We went to school, which was compulsory in Kingston. The elementary school had white teachers in charge, and there were Jamaican teachers. My first week was at Mico School, in January 1907, with a coloured teacher. We then were living in Rum Lane, behind the school which was in Hanover Street. That first week at school was my last with a native teacher. The second week started with a holiday on the Monday: Monday, 14 January 1907. A fine, sunny, tropical day; then in the afternoon around half past three the ground shook. It was the great earthquake. They say that there were three shock waves; certainly I remember the first. I was with another child and a more senior girl, who had been asked to take us for a walk. We felt this terrific vibration, and I looked round, and the girl had dropped to her knees and cried out 'Lord – have mercy.' That was the first prayer that I can remember, and it was said with such fervour and depth of feeling that I've never forgotten it. We were grabbed and rushed off, homewards; then mother appeared. Later we moved off to the racetrack and joined the people with their bundles of possessions. I can recall going to bed at the racecourse. There was a fire in the city, and the sky was red. We were there most of the next day, but we joined the drift back to the centre.

Of course I went, with other kids, to look at the damage, looking at the shambles that was left of Kingston. Most of the houses were bungalows, just one level, not at all high. There were two-storied and grander houses in the European quarter. The roofs had tumbled in; the wooden shingles were everywhere. Walls were crumbled. In retrospect, having the experience of the bomb damage in the 1939 to 1945 war, the way things were cleared up was somewhat comical: a chap with a wheelbarrow, here and there, taking debris away. When I was in Berlin in late 1945, in the Stars in Battledress military entertainment group, I saw the same chaos as the 1907 earthquake. One of that troupe, a Czech comedian who had worked in Berlin in the 1930s, was our guide, and our three-ton truck went all over Berlin. Lanes, just wide enough for our truck, were cleared through the rubble, bricks, and ruins. Mountains of rubble, just like Kingston in January 1907. I was too young to appreciate the mourning for the dead, but that must have affected a lot of people, for there were eight hundred dead in a city of around sixty thousand.

After the earthquake, or, more correctly, after some of the damage was repaired, I went to the Catholic school on Sutton Street. This was run by nuns from England, America, Cyprus, and Malta. Some had been in the West Indies long enough to have a Jamaican accent. They were very, very nice people. It was considered a good school. I must tell you that the influence of these Americans and English, was strong. Their kindness influenced our concepts of England – and America, too – as the mother country. After the six years of elementary education, if someone had pity, and you were sponsored, you could get to St George's College, the Catholic secondary school for boys. And there you had a chance at the scholarships which would take you for education in Canada, Britain, or the USA. But you needed money.

St George's had rivalries with the other colleges, such as Munro College and Wolmer's School. Generally these had more coloured pupils than the boarding schools in the country. In the late 1950s, when I was the warden at the Alliance Club in London, the Jamaican undergraduates who resided there were all from these colleges. Earl Thames, a Rhodes Scholar, had been at Wolmer's, I think. Anyway, he got a tennis blue; he changed his course, studied theology, and is now Reverend Thames. At the same time two other Jamaicans who were at the Alliance were Ken Whitborne, who became an optician, and Vernon Forbes, who studied at the London Bible College and was invited back to Kingston to be the headmaster of Munro College – from pupil to headmaster.

I can recall one neighbour in Rum Lane, an old Englishman who had 'gone native'. He was about fifty years old, and had resigned from being a European. He had a long beard, down to his hips: bearded men were very rare in Jamaica. He wore old clothes and was really tatty. Perhaps he had been a sailor. He was a nice man, and played with us children. We asked him questions on matters which puzzled us, and the neighbourhood regarded him as a seer. There was a half-caste lad, of around twenty, named Basil McMorris, and the two were friends. I recall the older man holding up the newspaper showing the headline that the *Titanic* had gone down, which was in April 1912. It was a big headline. Now the *Gleaner* cost a penny in those days, a lot of money, and few people in our district had it – maybe two or three. In fact, if you got hold of a copy it might be days old. That's how we had the news.

There were European children at the Sutton Street school because it was Catholic and because it had high standards. Five in a class of no more than thirty. Their parents lived in the district, but the best schools were in the country, and were boarding schools. Coloured lads with the best recommendations from their minister, whose parents had the money, could get into those schools from time to time. The white children at my school had their lunches brought by servants, and would be collected by carriage. At the top of Rum Lane there was an enormous house. It seemed enormous to me, then; certainly it had a swimming pool. It fronted on to Hanover Street. There were four or five children, and they joined with us in the lane, and in turn we would go into the grounds of their house. I can recall their mother, living within the racial stratifications expected – watching – arms folded. We black kids weren't unwelcome, but we weren't greeted in the most friendly manner either.

There were coloured businessmen; in fact such businessmen and landowners were not rare. The famous London doctor Harold Moody was the son of a chemist in central Kingston – I suppose he had qualified in Britain – certainly he must have studied pharmacy, otherwise he could not have dispensed his wares. Anyway, Moody's shop was right opposite the market, and the country people would bring their produce to town to sell, and take advantage of the trip to buy medicines and other goods which were impossible to obtain in the rural areas and villages. Moody's pharmacy was imposing. It was very busy, with sufficient staff to meet the needs of the customers. I understood that he had a very kind heart, and would take payment from country folk even if it was short of the real price. I don't know where the idea came from that his business did not survive the earthquake, for I recall it as a busy place after the city was rebuilt.[1] I don't recall seeing the statue of Queen Victoria which they say was turned on its base by the force of the tremor, but that may have been in Victoria Gardens, or at the seashore end of King Street where the passengers landed, and I didn't go there much.

There was a community spirit in our district, and so I suppose it was throughout Kingston. If a man was injured, and couldn't work, or was ill, or had bad luck, it would be known to everyone; and he would get coppers from the less well-off and silver from the rich. Those who had nothing were known to all the others. None of us had much. I can recall the Syrians, traders from Jordan and Lebanon I suppose, who hawked clothes from door to door. They always had a young Jamaican to carry the load. They would call, door to door, and give credit. Each week they would call for the payments. The Syrians were able, afterwards, in the 1920s, to open up shops in the city. Abject poverty had stunted the ambitions of Jamaicans; lethargy was encouraged by the environment. Beautiful scenery, the sea to swim in if you didn't mind the odd shark, and lush greenery outside the city. You could walk to the country in ninety minutes. As I've said, ambitious Jamaicans left the island. The weekend market showed Jamaicans with enterprise: small chocolate cakes of shredded coconut, on trays, brought in by the country women. Using all the enterprise and tiny cash reserves she had, shredding the coconut, and baking it in little cakes, walking twenty miles to sell for a few pence. Sometimes there would be four or five women selling the same thing – my, how they would look at each other. A twenty-mile trip, to compete with others, for pennies.

Women made clothes; they posed as dressmakers. I said posed because you had to see their creations to understand that it was an act. If you went to the high school you were expected to wear a uniform, and of course the scholarly but poor boy could not be so well presented as his fellows. A scholarship to such a school was a burden on the family if they were from a poor background. It was the fashion to wear white, and these poor lads had white uniforms that were washed in chocolate water. I mean, if they had been washed in chocolate water their uniforms would have been no darker. And holes in their stockings the size of an orange. You hardly ever saw children running about naked in Jamaica. Most of us were bare-footed; we had shoes, which would be brought out on Sundays, to go to

Linstead Market, 1909, wooden shingles, unpaved roads, typical of rural Jamaica.

church, or to parties. You would get a pair of shoes when you were ten, and three years later you were expected to wear them. So you would see chaps hobbling off to some event, their toes pinched and aching.

We did all right for food, for the country people would bring sweet potatoes, cassava, yams, breadfruit, and plantains to the markets in Kingston. Fish was fresh, really fresh, and the fish men would have agreed rounds; the same fellow would carry his catch round the same streets and lanes of an area. 'Fresh mullet' would be the cry. You would recognise the man's voice, the sound of his voice, and from that know it was the regular fellow. It wasn't like the 'cries of London' which I first saw in a music encyclopedia, and which you could still hear in London in the 1930s. Then there was dried salt cod which was imported and sold in huge barrels. Every Jamaican woman prides herself on her cooking skills with salt fish, peas and rice, and ackee. There were chickens, for eggs, and we kept them in our backyard, as did everyone I suppose. I was given a chick by my mother, and told to look after it. Can you imagine trying to recognise one chick from another? I can still recall the cackle when the hens laid. I used to get so busy playing that my mother had to send for me at meal times. My routine as a youngster was out into the yard and wash my face at the tap, off to school, then play until dinner, and play until bedtime. I wasn't keen on food, so I can't recall any meals or special dishes. And my father wasn't too good at looking after us after my mother went to the Canal.

The bread, in loaves much smaller than are sold in Britain, because none of us had much money, came from bakeries. Chinese people ran the local shops, on the corner. These fellows couldn't speak much English, but they befriended little children, who taught them how to read. You might think, if these Chinese and Syrians could squeeze a living in Jamaica, then why didn't the local people seize those opportunities. The simple reason was that there was no way for them to amass the necessary capital to make a start. Also the Syrians and the Chinese had come thousands of miles and they had pressures on them to try, try, and try again. And there was exploitation. By which I mean one Chinaman, who perhaps had come as a labourer, had opened a tiny shop, and he would bring in a relative who manned that shop whilst the first chap went out for merchandise and bargains. The poor fellow in the shop was worked like a slave by his smarter, more experienced, brother. With that sort of intense effort some Syrians and Chinese achieved. And off went the pigtail to show they had adjusted. I saw one or two Chinamen with pigtails. These Chinese traders aspired to have what would today be called small supermarkets at strategic spots in the city. Leahong used to have a tiny shop, but he arrived at Cross Roads, where everyone changed trams, which was not far from the army base up South Camp Road.

The army was at Up Park Camp; the parade ground had a panoramic view of sea. Well, from there to the city centre was twenty minutes. Leahong had a big shop at Cross Roads by the 1920s, an attractive shop, well-positioned. He was as English as a Chinaman could be. His children went to the local schools and then to college, for he had the money. There was one Chinaman who often got me to read out bits and pieces to him, and other children helped, and so he picked up English.

Economic circumstances held back the bulk of the people. Education was available in Kingston but after that, at whatever level, there wasn't much. Good luck was important: everyone was running, but there was only one winner. We thought of leaving the island. Get to Cuba and from there to the United States. Or to British Guiana, where you get into Venezuela. You had to get away from Jamaica to stand a chance. A family would save enough for a fare to New York and off went one member. In the USA one month's wages were the equivalent of a year's work in Jamaica. Work hard, save every penny. Write home, so every week a letter would be crossing the water to the family. And from savings in Jamaica and always from that first migrant, enough would be collected to pay the fare for another. Two people working, and sending, and bringing; and sending and bringing. The pull of America was tremendous. You could get a lump sum by joining the army, or the police, for there was a gratuity at the end of the term of service: the then-fantastic sum of £40. That would pay for fare and more. In America they took any kind of work – anything, it's a job. Responsibility to the family is a very powerful pressure and encourages stability. Young people here in London today wonder at the old West Indian street cleaners with their luminous striped coats, brooms, and pushcarts. Those fellows are from the country, arrived here in the 1950s, and took a job – any job, that gave them stability. From a London focus it is not much, but for people who had seen no other opportunity in their homeland, it is a real job. And for years they have been cleaning the streets. And so it was in the USA when I was a youth. I heard of people going to America all the time. It was a magnet. That's why Marcus – Marcus Garvey – went to America.[2]

In Jamaica ownership of land was an aspiration for all. Chaps who could scheme their way tried everything. Absentee landlords let them be their 'estate managers', as it were. And these fellows would rent out little houses which weren't owned by them. They had the power but not the title deeds. This type of landlord was seen in Britain in the 1950s, when the West Indians came here. Exploitation, of course.

The Chinamen got to know the people, and although they never gave credit they had a rapport with the city people and became successful in business. There were enterprising lads who had no money – not what you would call money – and somehow they represented British firms, and were agents for this, that, and the other. But I don't suppose they made a great deal of money, as there weren't many people to buy goods. The trams used to go up King Street, where all the prestigious shops were, to the Victoria Gardens, and east along East Queen's Street towards the country; if you went west, towards the European quarter, there were more shops. They sold imported merchandise, for I suppose nothing much was made in Jamaica apart from the rum. King Street had the post office, and the tax office, and other government buildings, facing each other, behind lawns, across the street. That's where the Armistice Day parade was held.

There were mixed race people – then they were called mulatta, half-caste, octoroon, or sambo. There were real divisions between white and black. These coloured people were often the results of liaisons between slave-owners and favoured women slaves, who would be transferred to a neighbouring plantation and kept as a mistress, with a brood of coffee-coloured children. And how such women regarded themselves: a higher rank than their sisters. That view of white skins is still current in Jamaica, I think. I experienced that, in Jamaica and also here in Britain, from the time I settled in London. Yes, I worked in London with coloured women and they would look right through you. The climb to the white was very important, and still is, even here in England. Every parish in Jamaica had its outstanding native families. Some of them were landowners, whose grandfathers had been slaves and had been given the land when the old slave-owner died. I remember in St Elizabeth there was the Hutchinson family, and I was there during my military days, when we were on a two-week camp in the country. The old man was owning a great big house, with stables, and servants. I had never come across that style – black people with that style – before.

There were tourists, mostly American, and they didn't trouble us. Cunard liners would come in periodically, and the Royal Mail Steam Packet Company's ships, two or three a week, would come and go. There were few black people in the crews of the ships to England, whereas the American ships would have the occasional Afro-American crewman, usually doing the dirty work. The banana boats had black crews and white officers. Qualified seamen were white, and in charge. There were very few motor cars when I was a lad. The Governor, the Colonial Secretary, some army officers and a few rich people had them. So the trams were used by everybody who had enough fare money. There were no racial distinctions on the trams, but people would avoid sitting next to Europeans, as this reduced the risk of a snub or an insult. But there again you might find that the fellow would start up a conversation. The drivers and conductors were usually natives, but never white, as it was not a job for Europeans.

Homes were lit by kerosene lamps, and the houses of the aspirants, those who aimed at European standards, would have three or four, with perhaps one suspended from the ceiling. Yes, plates were enamel: they chipped but didn't break or crack. There were no wild animals apart from the mongoose, which had been brought in to keep down the snakes and had been so successful that there weren't any snakes in Jamaica. The coat of arms of Jamaica shows a crocodile, but they had been decimated and I don't know of anyone who has seen one. Sharks were in the sea, as I've said. I learned to swim by watching the other lads on the beach. As a child, life was free. We played the same games as you here in England; you don't need paving stones to play hopscotch. We ran, and jumped, and there was skipping, and the maypole.

Cricket developed when I was around ten or twelve. Before the 1914–18 war an English cricket team arrived in Jamaica. The Jamaica team was really supported by everyone; we were keen patriots. You can see that style of support on the television today, when the crowd in India, and the Caribbean, really shows its opinion of the home side. Actually that Jamaican side was racially mixed. The Europeans were a little too successful in business, too podgy to run, you know. After that, cricket was taken up everywhere. And we had the Nancy stories: when the youngsters were with the elders the tales would be told.[3]

I had no ambitions and I would have drifted on I suppose, but for the influence of Mother De Chantal. It was 1912, after I had seen that headline about the *Titanic*. My mother was working in Panama, and I was too much of a handful for my father, so I was sent to the Alpha Cottage School, which was the Catholic orphanage in the suburbs of Kingston.[4] My first day at Alpha School was about to end. The Catholics had prayers and a hymn at the end of the day as well as at the beginning, and when that first day ended Mother De Chantal took me in and said 'We have a new member of the family.' My father had tried, but mother was away, and I was eleven and a troublesome lad. If it had not been for that good lady . . . It was the first time I thought, 'here I have a white mother.' We had white teachers, priests and nuns, and Father Williams suggested that I should think of becoming a priest and told me about a character named Father Rapael. He was a black priest in America.[5] I gave it some thought, but the major influence in my life in my years at the Alpha School was music, and I owe that to Leyland Palmer, who took me into the brass band which he led.

We had the Boy Scouts in Jamaica, and I had been a scout when I was at the Sutton Street School. The Alpha boys' band had a uniform similar to the Boy Scout uniform. That British influence was always so strong. There was Empire Day, 24 May. All the children wore white. We called it Bun and Cola day, as we would get that treat from the school. We would march, and sing 'Britons Never Shall Be Slaves'. Naive – such gusto – Britons never never will be slaves.

Talking of churches, it was true that certain pews were reserved for Europeans; it wasn't marked, but we all knew. I recall Holy Trinity Cathedral being built after the earthquake, and a chap painting high in the roof. Colonel Ward gave thousands to get the organ – a wonderful organ. The cathedral was well supported but there were local religious leaders, such as Bedward, who attracted the people, and would be the talk of the town for a while. Afterwards they would be immortalised in Jamaican folk songs.

When I was a little lad I would hear their singing, and see them with their Bibles and canes, and listen. All little kids love singing, and I would see them, and follow them to their hall, and listen outside. Now, here in Britain you see elderly West Indian ladies going to church, in their finest hats and gloves, but you didn't see that in Jamaica. They think that this is the correct thing to do, because their 'betters', the Europeans in Jamaica years ago, would wear hats and gloves. But not the Jamaicans then. How can I explain? The headscarf is the symbol of a working class woman, so they wear hats, here in England. And the dialect expressions which you can hear in Britain are corruptions of the old, posh English of the whites. 'Look you, here,' was a top-drawer expression when I was young, and it was copied and became 'Look oo, 'ere.' There must be others but I am so Anglicised that they have slipped out of my ken.

The roof tiles were wood, and corrugated iron was utilised only for the government buildings. There were some changes in the city as it was rebuilt after the earthquake, but not that many because it was a poor country. When I was in the army in 1921, with three other fellows I imported four bicycles, and would peddle round town when I was not in the barracks. There weren't that many cycles, then, and we were the envy of many. The bikes came from England and, with freight and import dues, cost about five pounds each. To travel meant that you walked, like those country people bringing produce to sell in the city markets. Who would take you? I was up on the north coast once, with a colleague in the army from there, during my annual fortnight's leave. We had a lovely time, but that was the first time I had been there.

I can well remember one Christmas. I mean just a single Christmas, when I was eight, nine, or ten. My mother had toothache and I was sent to King Street to buy some camomile. It was Christmas Eve, and the shops were open right up to midnight and later. So I got the camomile and was walking back – a scruffy, barefoot kid, when I looked in at the soda fountain where they sold sundaes. I was looking through the door at this group, and there was a woman, who was Irish, perhaps Scottish – certainly not English – and she had one of those toys you get from a cracker or from a party. You blow down them, and they unroll, and make a noise, and the end has a feather on it. She saw me, jumped down from her stool, and asked me if I would like it. I nodded, half instinctively. 'Take it,' she said. It was a memorable gift. My mother wasn't terribly interested – because of the toothache. We had small Christmas gifts at the school, which was nice. At Alpha we had a similar religious background, with midnight mass, and I well remember 'Silent Night'. We sang that lovely hymn every Christmas. When I got into the Alpha brass band we played at the garden parties on Christmas Day and Boxing Day, and got a good feeling from being part of those parties, too. Here in England the days have gone when you had big Roman Catholic processions. The brass band was very much in demand for things like that, the big eucharistic processions, with all the children dressed in white, carrying statues, and singing hymns.

The school brass band had been going for some time and one of the ex-pupils was Leyland Palmer, and he took us for music. He was no great shakes as a musician but he could teach, and he gave me Rimbault's *Catechism of Music*, a book priced at a shilling [5p]. I learnt most of my music from that. Later on I was given Longman's *Music Course*, a really thick book, from – from where I don't know. It was just what I wanted. The first musical fellow I can recall was Oscar Lecesne, who was at Alpha when I went there. He had this euphonium, and I kept looking at it, and he said I could have a blow, so I grabbed it and made a sound so quick and so loud that it qualified me for the band. I was inquisitive then, and that interest took me and made me investigate all the instruments, and learn to get a note or two from them. Nearly all the boys in the band had a piece of manuscript with all the fingerings of all the scales, and I got hold of that. So I learnt to play B-flat, the scale of B-flat. Then, being an inquisitive boy, I looked at the baritone horn, and saw that he was playing in the treble clef, and his scale was in C. But the fingering was the same, and when we blew together we were in harmony. So I could see that the music was written differently for some instruments. So I was learning the B-flat fingering in the bass clef, and the C fingering in the treble clef; and I tried it on the other horns, the tenor horn and the sax horn. And the next step was the cornet. Then I picked up a clarinet. I couldn't play it properly but by the time I left Alpha and joined the army I had five years' learning, after a fashion, all the instruments. There wasn't a stringed instrument in the brass band, but Alpha had a little string orchestra, and there I started to play the cello. We had violins, and from one I went to the next, and I picked up a bit here and there. So I could play all the instruments and read the sheet music for all the instruments, after a fashion, by the time I was sixteen.

The band had been fortunate, because the constabulary band had been disbanded and the captain, a chap called Ottley,[6] was Catholic, and he must have arranged for us to have their instruments, so we had almost a complete brass band and a lovely time. It was just what I needed. I was the euphonium player. And we had the assistance of the trained musicians of the West India Regiment band. Those soldiers would teach us and at the same time seek out talent for their military band. You had to be sixteen or so before you could join the army band, but that military influence started at Alpha School. At first I wasn't keen to join the army but I was told that promising musicians had the chance of studying in Britain, so I joined. Band Sergeant Ernest Beek, who had gone to England to study at the school of military music at Kneller Hall, helped me a great deal. He played the clarinet, and took a great deal of interest in me. So I joined the First Battalion, West India Regiment, in October 1917. Leslie Anthony Joseph Thompson, 6868.

Let me tell you something about aspects of Jamaican life, when I was a young man, before I start off on my military career. You know about ghosts, well in Jamaica we call such things *duppies*; and the element which you call witchcraft, and which is called *voodoo* in Haiti, is *obeah* in Jamaica. *Obeahmen* are supposed to know all the answers. Evil is real, you know, and if you have seen people who are supposed to have been affected by *obeahmen*, and are zombies, you would agree with me. Some of the *obeahmen* – some of them – had peculiar gifts. I agree with a comment I heard some weeks ago, that missionary societies should consider witchcraft in Third World countries, because it has a strength. What I recall is that I heard of an occasional person who had been affected to some extent. Two instances when I was in the army spring to mind. One chap had a swollen foot and there was no cure for him. And another chap's head grew: just like that, it got larger and larger. Evidence right in front of your eyes is difficult to dismiss. Oh yes, you could use *obeah* as a threat.

My mentor in the army band was 'Nimble' Callender, who had been to Kneller Hall in 1911, and was a good euphonium player. He was my target, and he helped me improve and I was quite good before I went to Kneller Hall. After I got back, I think it was, anyhow, we were in the barrack room, some forty or fifty men, and I was searching in my box for my stockings – my white stockings – to go on parade. They were missing and I yelled out 'Someone has got my stockings' and added that the *obeah* would be visiting them. Well, Callender threw them over to me in seconds. Oh yes, another time, in the 1920s, when I was playing in the orchestra at the Ward Theatre in Kingston, I knew a charming girl who sold ice cream there. She would wait, near to where I was playing, and when the break came she would walk up the aisle. She was the girlfriend of a married man, a sergeant – a cook – in the army. When he found out that we were pals he served me horrible food and gave me a rough time. However, his wife found out about the girl and things began to happen. The *duppie* was on her. Her mother took her away from the house. I went to the new place, and the three of us were there talking. Suddenly I was very tired and so I dozed off. Whilst I was sound asleep she had a terrible panic, really terrified she was, and there I was, just a few feet from her.

There were also the JonKanoo events, hardly a festival. There would be a horse's head and a sort of body – a stick for the body. And the children would ride it, but the affair got projected into the adults and they had dancing and singing. It was in Kingston, in a localised area: a neighbourhood or community gathering. There would be music, the 'mento' or calypso as it is called now. The participants were the poor – the working classes. I think the whole affair was very ridiculous. It had the atmosphere of a fair and, as with a fair in England you would get a certain type of person joining in, and others who were content to observe. The mento songs were rhythmic, and the words were on topical events. There was one about a racehorse named Barkwood – 'Barkwood belly like an iron bar' but pronounced 'a hiron bar'. And there was 'Slide Mongoose' which somehow became Sly Mongoose; and those songs, in the 1920s, were passed around and added to, and repeated, and eventually forgotten. I would think that Jamaicans were attracted by words, and would sing about someone or something.

In the First World War we had the same songs as in Britain, of course. As I've said, that British influence was so very strong. In fact, my very first stage appearance was at St George's College, at a concert organised by Father Pfister of Alpha School. Earlier he had put on Gilbert and Sullivan's *Pinafore* with the Alpha choir. Anyway, I had to sing 'Pack Up Your

Troubles in Your Old Kit Bag' at this concert, and I well remember that there was applause, clapping, between the verses, and Jacky Lewis and his pianist Amy Breakspear had to vamp, to keep the music going during this applause, until it had died down when the violin could lead in to the next section.

We had the British and American dance music in the 1920s, such as the Charleston and Black Bottom, but our people didn't go in for that dancing. It was more for the 'bright young things' who went to the Bournemouth Baths. As far as Jamaicans were concerned they danced quadrilles, which had been so well established over the years. Our army band played quadrilles and two-steps and that sort of thing. I can recall my mother having a practice dance: dances were so important then that you practised before you went to one. And, as a little lad, I watched my mother practising her steps: you chassé out and you turn here, and so on.

Oddly enough, the aspirants, who in so many ways were trying to be above the mass of Jamaicans and to be close to the Europeans, favoured neither in dancing. They had their position in society, but it was on the sidelines when it came to dancing. They were too superior to stoop to native dancing, and they disliked European dances. They were the middle classes, neither European nor natives. The average Jamaican would get up and enjoy himself when there was an opportunity, but the Europeans were too formal, and the aspirants were between the two.

When you went by tram along East Queen's Street you would pass the militia drill hall, and opposite was the European club. From five o'clock the whites gathered there for a drink. You could see that the only black people there were the waiters, serving the Europeans who sat drinking and talking. There would be an occasional dance at that place.

There were the usual entertainment spots of any port town. In Kingston, which had people close together, those who wanted to be distanced mentally from such whorehouses called them 'temperance bars'. What the French call the red lamp area. And sailors, European sailors, were there. You seldom saw Jamaicans – coloured lads – in those places, except as the musicians, for they had pianos and these chaps would play, by ear. Their repertoire was the current songs of the USA and also street music, and stuff from gramophone records. Some of the Alpha boys, who had picked up the odd hint about pianos, played there, and some of them developed a fine ear. My army work and the evening work at Movies and the Palace [theatres] in the 1920s kept me busy, and these lads would be working into the small hours when I was finishing in the pit and they slept most of the day, so our paths did not cross.

There were records in Jamaica, the best of the European masters, such as Brahms, and Chopin. Why there were no recordings made in Kingston is probably due to the small opportunity, and the lack of demand. It would perhaps take just one man with spirit and enterprise, and a recording company might have been willing to come from America or London. But that didn't happen to my knowledge.

I wasn't that keen on joining the army band but I was told that promising fellows went to Kneller Hall and so I joined up. There wasn't much of a risk being sent overseas although the war was on, because the First Battalion was guarding Jamaica. The Second Battalion had gone to East Africa and was then in Palestine with Allenby. I think the war had prevented some of the fellows going for training, for I was sent in 1919 and the previous batch had gone in 1911. Wington Thompson (oboe), Nimble Callender (euphonium), Alf Scott (trombone) and Edmund Ricketts (clarinet) had gone in 1911. Because Wington Thompson was already in the band I was known, after my army

number, as '68' Thompson. He became a lance corporal and
then was known as Cpl Thompson, of course.

We were soldiers, as well as bandsmen; we did square bashing, and the musketry course. In fact our instructor, an NCO,
had been trained in Britain, so that influence was there even in
small matters in the army. This fellow was a real Jamaican. He
was light skinned, but he didn't try to be white or copy the
English. For his language was real Jamaican, from the heart of
the country. He may have been in the regiment long enough to
have served in Sierra Leone, for the regiment had a long history. It was formed in America in the 1770s, and based in Sierra
Leone as well as in the various Caribbean islands. There was
another military group which has been confused with the West
India Regiment, and that was the British West Indies
Regiment. That was formed in 1915 and sent thousands of fellows to the war. Four lots of them went from Jamaica, and they
were cannon fodder.[7] They trained in England. They had
English uniforms, that greenish khaki colour. I don't recall any
of the BWIR joining the West India Regiment after the war
was over.

I well remember my first engagement with the regiment.
We had to play on board a visiting passenger ship, for a reception for some Americans who had been in Jamaica. They had
been around for some days and wished to repay some of the
hospitality they had received. I had only had my uniform for
one day and the buttons were none too clean. As I walked up
the gangway Band Sergeant Beek told me, in the most kindly
way, to always clean up my brass buttons before going on
parade. As a bandboy I was paid four shillings [20p] a week but
I had food, clothes, and quarters free.

There was a musical influence because of the war, for the
German commerce raider *Emden* had been caught in the
Atlantic and the officers were interned in Kingston, and were

in our barracks at Up Park Camp. Eight or nine officers were there, and they had a piano and a violin. One of the officers by the name of Straumann was a fine violinist, and he helped us with our music. Time was nothing to him. One or two of the others helped us, for they had all the time in the world. There was a German businessman with them, and he had a business in Harbour Street. I went to see him for a day job after the regiment was disbanded in 1926, but he said no.

During my service I got to know fellows from all over Jamaica. There was a mixture, with fellows from Barbados, too. Sgt Coward was from Barbados. We said Barbadian, which became Barbadjian, hence Bajun. There were odd chaps from other islands, and a half-caste fellow named Sgt Ainslie: he was born in Britain, I don't know where, though. The routine was musical after our basic military training. The band would rehearse in the morning, and after lunch we had individual practice, or studying for our army educational certificate. The Third section was really a primary standard; the Second was elementary; and the First – which was in two parts – was a basic standard. You were expected to pass, although we were not disciplined if we didn't. I passed my First. This education took place between two and four, with an army schoolmaster from England. We had two or three proper teachers, and one was a brilliant organist, and he used to play in churches all over the island. This Warrant Officer Lever had heard that I had some talent, so he called me up in front of the class, and asked me questions about chords and harmonies. I wasn't bothered in that way again, though. 'Last Post' was at ten, and 'lights out' at 10.15, so you had to have a pass to be out late. We were free to walk out from four o'clock most days.

There was other music in Kingston. When the Royal Academy and Royal College of Music of London organised the joint examination, the keen musicians of Jamaica had an

internationally recognised standard to aspire to and it was Vera
Manley who won a scholarship in 1908. Of course I didn't know
her then, but I got to know her and her husband Ludlow
Moody in the 1920s. Ludlow went off to study in London, too,
and had been acclaimed as a prodigy when he returned to
Jamaica with those excellent qualifications. Of course the government found him a job, as bacteriologist and pathologist, but
not where he was in charge of Europeans. The army was the
same, some of the officers who came from England had poor
qualifications. And better men, such as Ernest Beek, and – dare
I say it – myself, did the basic work.

Two people stand out in my mind as, shall we say, European
musicians, by which I mean capable of playing music of the
European classical tradition, to a standard found in Britain.
That suggests that Jamaicans had reserves of talent which
could be developed by the few who could seize the opportunity. There was Nation. Everyone called him Nation, which was
his surname. I think his first name was Harry, but I can't be
sure. He was brilliant, an excellent pianist. He had been to
Britain around 1908. He played the organ at Holy Trinity
Cathedral in Kingston, and at pontifical high masses. Nation
was well renowned as a player in Jamaica. I got to know him
after I returned from Kneller Hall, as my work with the regimental band left me free most evenings. By that time he was
quite a drinker. He would have been known to Vera Manley –
rather, Vera Moody. I don't know if she and Ludlow Moody got
married in London. Anyway, she was quite important in
European music circles in Jamaica in the 1920s. She was an
octoroon, aspiring, climbing to be white, you see. I am not sure
what she and Nation thought of each other.

The other, in a class by himself, was George Davis Goode.
He was a monumental man, in action and appearance, and he
directed choirs. He had massive concerts of choirs, performing

the sort of material that you would have at the Three Choirs Festival at Worcester and at Birmingham, at that time. He had his own supporters, and I suppose that the music was bought in advance and the ticket sales paid for the hire of the hall and for the orchestra. So his ventures were not too expensive to organise. He was a very hard worker, and it was much of his effort that enabled the Jamaican Philharmonic Symphony Orchestra to start in 1940. Perhaps he had studied in Britain.

I think that he had been abroad, either to America or to Britain, but he was so British that I can't believe it was to the States. Mind you, if he had a tutor in Jamaica then that fellow would have been first class. Goode had an excellent assistant named Sam Kitchin, a good right-hand man, with a fine voice, who was also very busy in the vocal music world of Jamaica. His son wrote a very nice article about me in the *Gleaner* when I went back to Jamaica in 1980. So, Jamaicans such as Vera Manley, Nation, and Goode could stand up and challenge any white performer of European music.

The military life suited me. People who haven't lived in an atmosphere of comradeship cannot understand that, for a youth of eighteen, it is pleasant: playing, learning, and getting paid; being with friends, and the exciting prospect of a trip to Britain. The war affected the Second Battalion, for they went off to Africa and fought hard against the Germans, and then to Egypt where they fought the Turks. I don't know if there was a large casualty list; I don't think so. But these chaps had travelled. They, and the BWIR fellows who had been in France and Italy, got back to Jamaica when I was in England in 1919. But when I got back to Kingston in December 1920 I found that they were very dissatisfied. The main reason was the black/white disparity. Just as in the Second World War, when British soldiers found out just how much money the Americans were getting for the same job. But it wasn't just the pay, I think.

They wouldn't talk about it, but one or two fellows would have a drink and a tale would be told. The two battalions merged. But I wasn't in Jamaica when these fellows got back and so I don't know what realities were behind their deep-seated resentment.

There was also the local music, the 'native music', which in those days was called the mento. It is funny how you hear calypso, but never mento. It's like Latin American music: you have a rhythm and sound that are of that music, no matter where you are in the whole of South America. And in the same way the mento of Jamaica was similar to the calypso of Trinidad. I agree that there was no carnival tradition in Jamaica, but if you heard the mento you would say 'West Indian' and so it was – different islands, different names. A few keys, and limited technical skills, but those fellows played right from the heart, and because of that feeling they were popular and their music was in demand for parties. I would go along and they would say 'Here's the professor coming, man.' The military band played the usual mixture: marches, quicksteps, and so on, just like brass bands and military bands in Britain. We played at official functions, at garden parties and parades, and so on.

2

Profession: Musician

I went to England with three colleagues. Two were cornet players and the other was a clarinet player: Arthur McClean and O'Connor, and the clarinettist was Milton Beckles. They returned to Jamaica and, as far as I know, never left the island after their military service. We caught a passenger ship to Avonmouth, in May 1919. We four lads were quartered amongst the crew – we were 'natives'. The crew were ordinary, plain, English fellows, with no prejudices, just working men. We talked, and asked them about Britain, and they asked about Jamaica. The night before we docked we were in the Bristol Channel, and we heard the water on the side of the ship, you know the way it changes when you are out of the ocean. That was early morning in late May, and it was light. We dressed and rushed up to have our first good look at England. There were bungalows and lawns along the river. My, how our fingers were numb after a while, because it is quite cold in the early morning. Then we were landing, and we could hear the shouts, and the ropes being thrown down. We went to the rail and looked down at the docks, where there were men talking. An Englishman – we could not believe this at first – in overalls, with a three-foot bass broom. An Englishman! We did not believe our eyes – having a job like that – it was a revelation to us. In Jamaica such work was done by natives; but in England the natives were white, of course.

We got our kitbags and went through customs, and our papers and Army paybooks were inspected. The trains came up to the ships; well, almost to the ship, and we could walk to the train. It was a lovely compartment, with curtains, and pillows, and cushions, and we four settled in and made ourselves comfortable for the journey to Paddington. A chap came in, and looked at our papers, and said 'Come this way, sir.' We were then told we were in the first class and that our authority was third class. We went off, humping our kitbags: no cushions, no curtains. And humbly we took our proper seats. We were met at Paddington by a bandmaster student from Kneller Hall – a Mr Seaman (he died at Kneller Hall: it must have been from gas or wounds from the war) who

Arthur McClean, *ca.* 1920

Milton Beckles, *ca.* 1920

took us via Baker Street to Twickenham, changing at Waterloo. At Waterloo we had a chance to stop at the military refreshment canteen, and there I had my first cup of tea in England. The woman had the spoon tied to the side, and she dipped the spoon in the sugar, and then into the tea. In Jamaica we have tea with our sugar, so – boy, what a taste. I think we all four left the mugs almost untouched. I was seventeen and in England.

The train journey to London was about one hundred miles across southern England but it is blurred in my memory. It was a kaleidoscope. But I well remember the light bulbs on the walls of the underground railway in London. They appeared to rush towards you and then pass you, but, of course, it's the train that is moving. I still look at those bulbs when I travel on the London tube. Kneller Hall is an imposing building, for it was the old home of the painter Sir Godfrey Kneller a couple of hundred years ago. Back in 1919 it was in the heart of the countryside, for London's suburbs had not spread that far west and Whitton was a tiny village then. We had to walk into Whitton, crossing the junction of five roads near the hall, to get to the post office, the greengrocer, and the tuck shop where we could purchase sweets. At the hall the students were accommodated at the back, in the newer part. We were on the seventh floor, and we had the only room with a fire. That was because we were from the tropics, I suppose. Sharing the room and that coal fire were other students. I recall one fellow named Atkinson, and Jock Rainey, a fine cornet player who was a lance corporal in the Royal Scots.

We had been issued with British-style warm uniforms in Kingston, because in Jamaica, unless we were on parade, we wore shorts. There was no special uniform at Kneller Hall, for we were proper soldiers and had our own regimental uniforms. On parade there were all colours and styles; it was very picturesque – especially the kilts worn by the Scots. There were around five hundred of us although the hall could take up to seven hundred. But the war was still on, for the peace treaties were not signed until June 1919, and certainly there was fighting in Russia and in Ireland, and chaps serving in Germany. Some of my colleagues did not have full dress uniforms because of the wartime shortages. That war of independence in Ireland killed some of my pals, chaps I met at Kneller Hall, for there was no exemption from fighting for army bandsmen, and so they served with their regiments. That ended their letters to me in Jamaica. But that was far from what was in our minds in 1919, of course.

There were concerts each week at Kneller Hall, in the summer, on Wednesday afternoon, except the last one which was in the evening. In the open, on the tiers of the bandstand, we looked very colourful. There was a lot of local support, so these concerts were popular, and we kept a high standard. Our teachers were in the army, with permission to be away from their regiments, to teach at Kneller Hall. There were more clarinet tutors than any other instrument, as there were more clarinettists in a military band. Indeed, our bandmaster in Kingston, Stanley Owen, was the son of a professor of the clarinet at Kneller Hall, although he had retired by the time we got there. Stanley Owen played the bassoon, and he was one of those failures, by which I mean that he had been found the job in Kingston after he had failed his Kneller Hall examinations. There was no second chance at them, and how could you return to your regiment? So they found positions for these failures in the military and police bands in Africa and the West Indies.

There were three clarinet tutors, and two for the cornet – Lambe, and Leggett of the Coldstream Guards. One for the trombone, and one for the euphonium. My tutor – the euphonium professor – was a dapper little fellow of around fifty named Edwards. He was very pleasant, and when I won the silver medal he was overjoyed, for his name went up on the board as my tutor. Now Callender had been my target back in Kingston, and I had put in lots of practice when I was off duty, and I had studied Longman's *Music Course*, which had given me a thorough understanding of the theory of music. I was probably well ahead of regimental standards when I left Kingston. At Kneller Hall I found that theory to be a godsend. I played with cornet and clarinet players, and got a broad experience. Actually I had been able to play all the brass instruments when I was at Alpha, as well as the cello and the clarinet, and I had picked up the violin and percussion at Up Park Camp. You see, I was curious and I would ask my colleagues about their instruments and they would show me, and so I picked up bits here and there. Of course the percussion in those days was just side drum, bass drum, and cymbal – not the factory you have today. Well, because of my studies of that book I sailed through my theory examinations in England. Actually there was no need for a bandsman to have much theory, for that was required of bandmasters, who were first class warrant officers. I remember once in the practice room, when we were playing the developing section of the overture from Gounod's *Mireille*, the director stopped us and asked the euphoniums what they were playing. I spoke up and said 'A pedal note for sixteen bars', The other fellows laughed, for it is an odd name, I suppose. Well, the director told them 'He's quite right, you know,' and after that I was well respected.

We four Jamaicans were respected by our fellows. They were the salt of the earth, real Tommy Atkins fellows, with no front. We were all nicknamed 'Darkie' but it was with affection, not to be offensive. The only thing any of them knew about Jamaica was rum. Some of the lads idolised us, and we became mascots in a way. There was an Irishman named Ferguson, a euphonium player, mad keen on soccer, and he and I were close friends. And I remember one Sunday concert when I had to play the solo in 'Ave Maria', the director put down his baton and applauded me, too. Right in front of the whole band.

The building was cleaned by local people, and we called them swags. One swag, about my age, was Bill Slaughter, and he cleaned some of the offices, and the stairs. It was in October 1920 that I was going down stairs when he called me into an office. At that time the professors were making their recommendations, if any, regarding the prizes and the medals. There was complete secrecy, but Slaughter had seen a confidential letter and told me that I was down for the silver medal, and that I shouldn't tell a soul. I kept quiet about it. The Commandant gave out the prizes at the end of term: the band sergeant called out the names. A short fellow named Marks got the bronze and then my name was called out. The boys stamped their feet and shouted out 'Good old Tommo.' I thanked the commandant, and turned to the assembly and thanked them for their support and comradeship.

I regret that I did not take advantage of the opportunities to see anything of England, but I was concentrating on my studies. I did go to the theatre in London, seeing *Rose Marie* at Drury Lane. I also went to the Lyceum, to see a pantomime with Ali Baba and the thieves. Of course I was in uniform. I was in the dress circle: everybody looked at me, for they were not used to seeing coloured people. I had purchased a nice box of chocolates, but I tipped them over, right in the middle of a quiet moment. All those eyes, looking at me! In the interval I could hear people walking on my chocolates.

O'Connor left England early, with some problem with his eyes, and he had left the army by the time I got back to Kingston at the end of 1920. There was a two-week break at Kneller Hall at Christmas, but those with nowhere to go remained behind. We were allowed to go out every day. Arthur McClean made pals with a family at Heston, and he used to go there. He often took my slippers, without asking, when he was off there. He had become friendly with this girl, and her mother liked him, too. Milton Beckles was a keen card player, and he played poker with the lads. We could play games, but I don't

recall any cricket although we worked throughout both summers. Between noon, when band practice ended, and two,
when the next practice started, you had time for lunch and
fooling around.

At Kneller Hall one of the English students told me that I
ought to hear the Southern Syncopated Orchestra. In fact, he
thought that I would know them as they were the same colour
as me. They were Americans, and this orchestra and choir were
having a great success at the Philharmonic Hall near Regent
Street in central London. This was the first opportunity that
Londoners had to hear jazz actually played.[1] Will Marion Cook
was the musical director, I believe, and he was replaced by
Egbert E. Thompson. I never did go to see them, but I met
Egbert Thompson in 1924, as I'll tell you.

I did go to the Albert Hall, to the ballad concerts, and there
I also heard *Hiawatha* by Coleridge-Taylor. Now I knew that
Samuel Coleridge-Taylor was coloured; I don't know how, but I
knew; and I was elated, proud of his success. Indeed, my ticket
was given to me by someone who was at Kneller Hall, probably
knowing that I was the same colour as Coleridge-Taylor. Of
course, I went. I didn't see any other coloured person there.

I was friendly with a student from the Seventh Dragoons
named Gregg. I was an infantryman and so was fascinated by
the cavalry. He and I went up to London, to pass the time, one
Saturday, and I was wearing his cavalry breeches. We got off the
train at Waterloo and walked towards the river. Because the
Union Jack Club attracts servicemen the area was a favourite
for redcaps – the military police. Crossing the bridge I saw two
redcaps, and I told Gregg to walk on as I would pretend we
were not together. So he did, just as I feared, these two burly
military policemen walked across to me. 'What's your name?'
they asked. They had looked me up and down and I think they
had seen I was not correctly dressed. I spoke in gibberish –

'Ugga mugga hoobie dah dah laar.' Real rubbish, but I kept at it when they asked me a few more questions and they thought I couldn't speak English, and so off they went.

I got used to the meat-and-two-veg style of meals in England, but I never thought much of it because in Jamaica we had spices, fried the food, and mixed all vegetables and bits together, making it tasty. But we were lads and had healthy appetites and just got used to it. There were no records at Kneller Hall, and any music was from us. And there were no dances.

I had an invitation to tea, which was really quite funny, and certainly an experience. First you have to realise my position. The Europeans in Jamaica had lawns, and we lads could see them at night, with dinner jackets and best dresses, through the large windows or having a smoke or meal in the garden. It was so much part of everyday life that they were taken for granted. We did think it was odd to have tea – a hot drink – on a hot afternoon in the garden, because if we had any spare cash we would have sundaes. We knew that tea drinking was a European custom so we gave it no more thought.

Shortly after I arrived in England I went down to the village tuck shop and to the fruit and vegetable shop next door. The owner was a godly woman and it was a pleasant shop, and I bought fruit there. Her daughter was named Biddie, and she spoke to me, and asked me if I was busy on the next Sunday. And as I wasn't she asked me to tea. That Sunday afternoon the whole of Whitton made an excuse to call on that house. Eventually tea was served. I was taken into the dining room where the table groaned under the weight of plates, cups, saucers, cakes, biscuits, and buns: all those sandwiches, and scones, and so on. The mother picked up a jug and asked me if I took milk, and I said that I drank milk but why was she asking, and she told me that English people have milk in their tea. Then I was asked if I took sugar, and I told her that I did and that it came from Jamaica. I began to realise that having tea in England is a ritual, a custom. Hold your cup, take bird-like sips from the tea. Tear off a morsel of cake, and eat it. It is not a meal, but a chance for a chinwag. The atmosphere was frozen, the room was quiet, and no one was relaxed, until the mother – who was sitting opposite me – asked if she could touch my hair. She did, and remarked 'Just like a golliwog.' Biddie did the same. And that thawed the gathering: and so I was accepted. Everyone had been on their very, very, best behaviour; now it became comfortable. I thought then that if I ever had to leave Jamaica I would settle in England amongst such decent, polite, and kind people.

I had good memories to take home with me. Of course I did not know England, or the English, and my impressions were very undeveloped. The military life and uniform had protected me. Mother De Chantal had mothered me but had told me to go forward. Stanley Owen, my first bandmaster, had also been very encouraging. All the Kneller Hall people – students, clean-ers, kitchen staff, and tutors – were so nice. Which reminds me that, doing some spud-bashing in the kitchen I cut into my left hand index finger and thought that I would have to stop cello playing, but the treatment worked (although I still can see the scar). And I never had to work in the kitchen again.

I recall walking out with some fellows, in the apple orchards around Twickenham, when two small chaps, seeing my black face, egged each other on until one rushed up and asked me the time. When I replied he returned in triumph to his pal and said that I did, indeed, speak English. And when we went into Twickenham to the cinema, which would be around five or five-thirty, a lot of faces would be pressed against the glass in the shops as I went by. They hadn't seen black faces before, you see.

I asked the Director about any possibility of becoming a bandmaster, and he advised me to talk it over with my commandant in Kingston, whose recommendation would be necessary. We got back to Kingston on Christmas Day, 1920; the news of my success and the medal had gone ahead. I told the lads that I wanted to be a bandmaster, and they laughed: fetch a copy of *King's Regulations*, they said. And there it plainly was written that anyone above the rank of warrant officer, third class, had to be European. After more than sixty years I still believe that the Kneller Hall Director told me that because he wanted to soften the blow, knowing that it would be easier for me to accept back in Jamaica. Certainly the irrevocable nature of army rules was known to me. I must admit that I was naive. Indeed, I was a silent one.

My education, or rather my political education, changed around 1921. Lance Corporal Edmund Ricketts was far older than me: he was a mature thinker. I'm sure it was through him that I read a copy of *Negro World*. Garvey had gone to New York and there founded the Universal Negro Improvement Association, or UNIA. Each week they published the *Negro World*. Certainly Ricketts had other American newspapers (he went to Canada in 1926 and led a band, which broadcast from Toronto in the 1930s) and I think it was from him that I got my copy. I had no colour consciousness, but reading *Negro World* punctured my thinking. In Jamaica we had been duped; no, given a palliative, so that we accepted a peaceful and uneventful life. A radical was needed, and Marcus Garvey was that man. Why should there be such divides between the races? I could see the poverty in Jamaica, the houses falling down: Garvey made me see. I had expected high standards in England, and I saw them there. In Jamaica I expected no changes, but Garvey made me ask why not. Why all those dinner jackets, all dressed up, that level of wealth and all the poverty around. There was a need for changes, and it was Marcus Garvey who alerted me to that need, and to the disparity that existed.

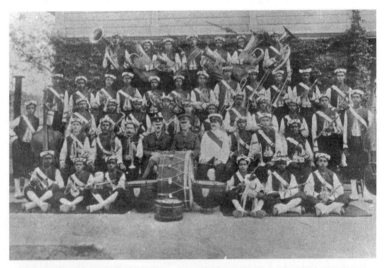

West India Regiment Band, Kingston, 1922: the group that went to Toronto, taken outside the officers' mess at Up Park Camp.
Left to right:
Back row: Spencer, unknown (brass bs); 'Nimble' Callender (euphonium); Dm Sgt Jacob 'Spud' Murphy; 'Chappie' McClean, 'Affu', unk. (brass bs).
2nd row: unk. (d); Porteus (cl); Arthur McClean, Leslie Garrel (cnt); 3 unks. (saxhorn); Adrian Walters, unk., Alan Weston (tbn); 2 unks. (cl).
Standing left: Leslie Thompson (string bs).
Middle row: Roland Rainford, Joe Appleton (sax); Heywood (bassoon); Willie McClean, unk. (cnt); Oswald 'Ozzy' Stewart; 2 unks., Drummond (cl).
Standing right: Forde (string bs).
Row with officers: Frank Dyson (dm), Edmund Ricketts (cl), Sgt Neilson (cnt); major leader; unk.; bandmaster 'Paddy' Nash; Delgado (bs cl); Richard Ewart (cnt), Sylvester Cork (cl).
Front row: unk., Henderson, Leslie 'Jiver' Hutchinson (cnt); unk., Louis Stephenson, 'Fitz' Knibbs (cl).

At Up Park Camp there were Europeans – I mean that British line regiments were there, with responsibilities to protect the island and to be ready to rush off to deal with any threat. And these troopers were white, of course. Well, the authorities in their wisdom wanted to deal with matters in a proper way, so the latrines were segregated. The lavatories sat twelve or sixteen at a time, but there was a dividing line – there were signs 'Europeans Only'. So the white fellows could not be polluted in the latrines by the black fellows, or the other way round! And those signs were not seen outside the Camp; and only in the lavatories in the Camp. From early childhood our mental outlook had been conditioned in such a way that a white person was always accepted as a superior so these signs were not offensive, which seems strange today. That acceptance of the 'superiority' of the white race stayed with me right until I began to hear about what Marcus Garvey wrote and said, and then I became aware of what discrimination means.

My routine after our return in 1920 was an hour's rehearsal before breakfast at 7.30; band practice from nine until noon; lunch break from noon until two; and practice or walking out until four o'clock. I taught privately. Here I must confess that I regret that I did not go back to teach the lads at Alpha; indeed, I abandoned them when I left for England in 1929, instead of staying and teaching what I knew. I told them that when I went back to Alpha in September 1980. However, from 1921 I taught small groups theory, for I could play the piano a bit; and I taught a group of violinists. I got £1 for an hour.

Over the years, from my days at Alpha up to the time I left Jamaica for London in 1929, I had contacts with veterans of the West India Regiment. Sgt Uriah Kknibbs – his two sons were bandsmen – had started the brass band at Alpha at the beginning of the century. It had been a drum and fife band before that, but they got real instruments, and Knibbs was involved at that time. Poor man – he had to write out each band part by hand. He was a flute player, as was another retired band sergeant by the name of B. De Cordova Reid (B. De C. Reid). He mixed in the community and directed choirs, and they did proper stuff, including cantatas. I played with Reid at some of those civilian concerts.

I knew Sgt Gordon as well. He had won the Victoria Cross

in the First Battalion, West India Regiment, in Africa.[2] He lived on War Department property when I was in the army, up near the firing range. It was a grace and favour arrangement, for Gordon had the respect of everybody. After all, the Victoria Cross is Britain's highest award for bravery. So, Sgt Gordon, who was in his fifties, was put in charge of the firing range. No one can steal a firing range of so many acres, so it was a nominal job. And he lived free of charge. To get to his home he had to pass the bandroom, so we saw him often. The new recruits were told about him, of course – 'That's Sgt Gordon, V.C.' He had a full military funeral when he died, which was in August 1922. Actually all the old soldiers had proper funerals, for I must hand it to the authorities at that time, for no old soldier, no matter how short his service, had a pauper's funeral. The island wasn't that big, and no veteran could die without the news reaching the authorities, and they took care of everything.

The two battalions merged and although Owen was a fine fellow the other bandmaster, Paddy Nash, was more senior and was kept on. Nash had none of Owen's panache. He knew of my skills and so he got me to do much of his work, arranging music for the band, writing out the parts, and so on. In 1922 we got the *Canadian Planter* and sailed to Montreal, and from there we went by train to Toronto, where we played for two or three weeks at the Canadian National Exhibition. It was in the summer of 1922. We were in a hotel, not a barracks. There were bands from all over the place, from all over Canada and the USA. The best was Creatore and his band: an Italian group from the States. Boy – what a terrific standard! Really it was amazing to have a band of that quality. I can recall their trumpeter playing the solo from the sextet of *Lucia di Lammermoor*: impeccable. We tried to take that standard back to Jamaica with us. We were the only coloured band there. The Canadians were nice and friendly; but of course we weren't looking for adverse elements.

In Kingston we used to play at the officers' mess, on Wednesdays and Fridays, and that kept us to a high standard, as we never knew who was there: a visiting naval officer, someone from one of the British regiments in Jamaica, or an important fellow on his way from Australia to England. The people came to the boundary fence of the camp to listen, too, so we had a good audience.

Because that stick-wagger Paddy Nash used me to do his work I was free most evenings, and I spent a great deal of time working in the cinemas of Kingston. There was no soundtrack with movies until 1929, and the moving picture houses used bands, of varying sizes, to accompany the film. The grander the theatre, the larger the band. At the Palace Theatre I worked with seven fellows – cornet, clarinet/saxophone, trombone, alto saxophone, violin, piano, string bass and drums. Some of these cinema musicians were ex-West India Regiment; they had completed their service. The trombone and clarinet players were ex-army; others were also civilians, and two (drums and bass) were from Alpha. There were lots of musicians in Kingston, for the army had had two bands, each of eighty musicians, and there had been a police band. It was around this time that I did arrangements for George Goode.

Movies had a duo, violinist Jacky Lewis and a Mrs Verity (piano), until I joined them with my cello. Jacky was the most celebrated violinist in the West Indies, and I remember him coming to play for us at Alpha and they were there when I made my first stage appearance. At that time his pianist was Amy Breakspear, who died very young. Jacky Lewis had a very large reputation. Mrs Verity, who was lighter than Jacky, had two or three sons, and Jim Verity took up the violin and went to England to study at the Royal Academy. In fact I met him there in the 1930s and we were in the same orchestra at the Adelphi, at His Majesty's, at the Drury Lane, and at the Palace at Cambridge Circus. He was active in music in London until after the war, when he returned to Jamaica. He set up a school of music in Kingston; in fact, there was some story of me joining him, but when I read about it it was news to me! Jacky Lewis and Mrs Verity played for years, and they had their own supporters, who would go to their recitals. At Movies, at Cross Roads, they gave a recital, providing a musical interlude in the film show, in the same way that big cinemas in Britain had those huge electric organs in the 1930s. Jacky Lewis was a civil servant, in the Treasury, and he was a settled fellow.

There was another violinist in Kingston, an English fellow named Willie Brown, whose standard was good and so he deputised for Jacky. Willie Brown's father was from one of these railway towns in England, perhaps it was Swindon – and he had taken up a position as an engineer in the Jamaican railway. He had some connection with music, for I can recall that they had a C cornet, an old thing, which Willie finally let me

Movies Theatre, Cross Roads, 'a brilliant centre of gaiety' (courtesy National Library of Jamaica).

play. Willie qualified as an accountant, got married, and settled down in Kingston, where he was active in music. Actually he was a rival to Jacky Lewis, in a way. Willie Brown was in an orchestra, an all-white affair, which had been set up, I think, by Jock Howie. Jock had served in the Green Howards, one of the British regiments stationed in Jamaica, and he took his discharge in Kingston. In fact Jock Howie directed orchestras at the Palace Theatre at the time I played with Jacky Lewis and Mrs Verity at Movies. A Jewish lad named Cox and some others got a dance band together; I remember that it was subtitled 'Dispensers of Aristocratic Jazz', which identified it as white. It was a dance orchestra, and they played at the Bournemouth Baths, outside Kingston, where you could drink and lounge by the seaside. They had a piano, a drum, a bass, a guitar or banjo, and Jock Howie was playing his trumpet, Cox played the violin and Willie Brown played both saxophone and violin. Cox and Brown played at the European club, but native bands got in there from time to time.

I don't recall any other local, Jamaican, bands playing that dance music in the 1920s. The hotels were in Kingston, at that particular time, for the Montego Bay area was not developed as a tourist resort; besides, Jamaica isn't that large, and so the tourist excursions left from Kingston. The Myrtle Beach Hotel had a dance, once a week, in the off-season. It was patronised by whites; blacks were waiters. And in the tourist season the American bands came down. It was usual for bands, in the 1920s, to be brought in from America, but the local boys got in, maybe, once a week. Actually there were few orchestras, dance orchestras, in Jamaica; regular work was in the cinemas. Dance groups were in the hotels, playing the popular music – requests – of the time. Such groups from America were always white. Jamaican bands were stop gaps, and were pick-up groups, apart from Howie's band at the Bournemouth Baths. So we

Granville
Campbell,
ca. 1940

Jamaicans aimed at the regular work in the cinemas. Mind you, years later, after the war, music in the hotels took off when Jamaican musicians came back from abroad, from war service, and had the strength of purpose to go to the hotel management and offer their services.

Looking at this old *Who's Who, Jamaica*, I see Granville Campbell's picture. I'd forgotten about Granville. He was a light-coloured Jamaican with a fine voice – a tenor. Yes, as it says here, he was the Caruso of Jamaica. He used to be employed for parties. Somebody would want to have a party, and they would ask the hotel to arrange something, and the manager would contact Granville. He was a pianist, a fine pianist, too, you see; and he would get four or five or six others. I used to play my cello with him. We played from sheet music, of course. This was even whilst I was in the regiment. Now most of the good fellows worked for the moving pictures, so Granville always had a pick-up band. At the end of the session he would be given an envelope, which contained the cheque, and he would put it in his pocket, telling us that he would change it – I'm still waiting for my pay! An evening with Granville – no money, usually. He came to

England, in the forties, but it was too late. Yes, this book does-n't mention the trip, so it would have been after the war. He was too old – born October, 1892. Oh yes – thirteen children: Granville was very prolific.

I also remember that there was a little fuss about Marie Lawrence in the *Gleaner* in the early twenties. I had been in England, and it interested me to read that she had performed at one of the Lyons Corner Houses – those inexpensive restau-rants in London at that time – and this report seemed to indicate that this was a very prestigious job. An Englishman wrote in and pointed out that the Corner House restaurants were second-rate eating places; he really had a dig at the Jamaican innocence, reporting that she was doing so well in London. That would have been, I suppose, around 1923. I never met her in England but I can well believe that she was here in the thirties.

That American magnet was still pulling Jamaicans away from the island in the 1920s. Indeed, hardly anyone thought of going to England unless it was on a scholarship, or to study law or medicine. Ordinary working chaps thought of America. It cost ten pounds to get to Cuba, and from there to Florida was easy. The Canal had been completed at Panama, but some Jamaicans went there to work in the hotels. Some time between my return from England and the break-up of the reg-iment in 1926 I read in the *Gleaner* that a Jamaican named Louis Drysdale had settled in England before the war and had become a voice coach, and that he had recently taught Florence Mills, the famous Afro-American singer. She had been in one of those New York shows around 1922, by Eubie Blake and Noble Sissle. Wington Thompson went off to New York and joined Blake; he was always reading American papers.

In 1924 we went to England, where we played at the British Empire Exhibition at Wembley.[3] We were accommodated at

The West India Regiment band, Wembley, 1924, *Left to right*:
Front row, Leslie 'Jiver' Hutchinson, Frank Dyson, Jacob 'Spud' Murphy, Cecil
Forde, Arthur Knibbs, bandmaster Thomas Turner, Sylvester Cork, 'Fitz'
Knibbs, Leslie Thompson (with string bs).
Second row from front: Sgt Neilson, Edmund Ricketts, Roland Rainford,
Oswald Stewart, Richard Ewart, unk., Milton Beckles, Egbert 'Piggy' Elliott,
Altamont Da Costa.

Mill Hill barracks in north London and were driven to the
exhibition grounds. I played the string bass. We were very popular, because of our Zouave uniforms,[4] and people would say
'Felix kept on walking'after the cartoon cat which was popular
at that time. And I remember playing 'Yes, We Have No
Bananas'. And at that exhibition we saw Africans for the first
time which, as Jamaicans, was very interesting. I don't have any
recollection of the Guyanese militia band which was there, but
it was a busy exhibition with thousands of people, and I guess
everyone with a camera took a picture of us.

At the Wembley exhibition a Jewish businessman from
Kingston, a very nice fellow, arranged a private function, a

party. The pavilion where Jamaican products were on show was used, and the Prince of Wales was invited along with all manner of important people. Well, whenever there is royalty there have to be soldiers and a guard of honour, and our band was invited to play at this party, so we formed a guard of honour. We didn't have fixed bayonets, of course, but we lined up and the Prince inspected us in the usual way. One of the brass bass players was nicknamed 'Chappie' and he had somehow got three medals. The lads who had been in the Second Battalion had fought in what was then called Tanganyika [Tanzania] and in Italy, and they had war medals. You can see them on the photograph. Two clarinet players, two brass bass players, and a couple of others had these medals. Chappie McClean was wearing his – not just the ribbons – and as the Prince passed along he stopped and chatted to him. Chappie was a very dark man, much older than the rest of us, so maybe he had served in Sierra Leone, just as Ottley had. Anyway, that was an honour for us – the son of the King of England had spoken to one of us.

Now we had a lance sergeant named Richard Ewart, who had been in the band for years. Dickie Ewart was a light-coloured fellow, none too brilliant as a musician but excellent as a barber. He used to cut the hair of the officers, and eventually he set up a barbershop: he died in a car crash. Anyway, he had been around for years. Yes, one retired major came up to us at Wembley and Dickie remembered serving with him years before. Anyway, Egbert Thompson came over from Paris where he was running a music agency, supplying musicians – coloured musicians. Actually he came with a bunch of them, to recruit from our band at Wembley. Dickie knew him, and some of the others had heard of him. Thompson was the son of a sergeant in the regiment, born or brought up in Sierra Leone. He had been to Kneller Hall in the late 1890s, but he went off to New York after his service career was over, and there he had become well-known and successful. I believe he had served in the US army in the war, and he had been in the Syncopated Orchestra in London in 1919, too. Thompson, like Dickie, was a trumpet player. They told us of the work and pay available in the commercial music world of Paris, and I recalled that five years later, and that was another reason for my migration to England.

These trips to Canada and England were too short to take a good look at the realities of life, and we were sheltered in the army. In 1924 I was still a bandsman, but that changed in late 1924 or early 1925. A group of lads went off to Kneller Hall after we got back: Eldon Stewart (trombone), two cornet players, one of whom was named Cacelard, and a clarinettist named Clunis. Well, Stewart, whose father had been a sergeant, was pushed by his father (who worked for the army's mineral water factory) and he became a lance corporal. He was driven on, and he pushed us – put us on fatigues. So I told him that if I was to cut the grass then he would have to do the bandmaster's work as that was given to me. He was a damn nuisance. Fellows said that Eldon Stewart was 'too damn regimental.' So I got up and requested to be considered to be a lance corporal. I got the promotion that very afternoon. By this time our band-master was Thomas 'Crutch' Turner – I've got a music book I bought from him, years ago. He had taken over from Nash, and had continued to let me do all the arranging. Now the band ser-geant left, and although Stewart was more senior I was made band sergeant, because I had the medal and the army education certificate. Crutch was mad, and stormed down to the office and got them to change it, and so Stewart became band ser-geant. I was demoted to corporal, which suited me, as the band sergeant's job meant that he had to be with the band all the time it was playing. So I was Cpl Thompson, 6868. And I still didn't have to go where the band went.

In 1926 the band became the Jamaica Military Band, for the West India Regiment was broken up. They say that the reasons were economic, but I think that the people in authority could not rely on the West India Regiment to be a reliable force in its police role, by which I mean keeping law and order and especially dealing with uprisings in Africa, which was why it had been stationed in Freetown, Sierra Leone. What a lot of people don't know is that many years ago, well over a hundred years ago, the West India Regiment had been formed and had six or seven battalions, and these were spread around the different islands of the British West Indies, and in western Africa as well. And in all that going around the influence of the men was brought with them and left behind them. Some of the fellows came back with African wives, and I have been told that Africans joined the regiment out in Africa. With that, and the Chinese and Indian labourers in the Caribbean, there was quite a mixture. At one time there was some advertising for people who would be prepared to leave Jamaica and go out to Africa, and one fellow who had been in our band took up the offer. In fact there were three of them, but I forget where they went exactly, but it was West Africa. I don't know what they did out there, but they duly did a tour of three or five years. I met the fellow, when he was back, and he said that things were not too good out there. Anyway, from 1926 there was no regiment: and that's when I went to the German fellow in Harbour Street to see if he had a day job.

I was involved with the music for the Ward Theatre, where proper touring companies, on their way to Australia most probably, would give a couple of weeks' performances – shows and plays that were running in London, really top quality acts. I had quite a lot of work in the cinemas, and after my army career was over in 1926 I took this up full time. Now, many of the moving pictures came from America, but all of them would come with cue sheets. As music director I had to read these cue sheets, and get the right sheet music ready, and write it out for the lads – ten seconds here, thirty seconds there, and so on. I had to get the music from my own collection, or from London or New York if there was a special theme. It was the same all over the world at that time. I had to direct the band, tell them when to change, and until I had seen the film this was guesswork assisted by the cue sheets. There were three or four pages to a cue sheet. My job was anticipating what would happen next on the screen. I wasn't always successful, for I well remember one film, which was set in Vienna. Every so often the picture would be of a dance scene, with 'Blue Danube' waltzing and typical Austrian classical music; that sort of thing. And then – back to the heroine – and back to the villain; and then a few seconds of the waltz. I had to get the lads to play that waltz for those two or three bars. Boy – what a task. After the first show the manager told me that I had made a real mess of it, for every time the girl spoke, my band played the waltz, and every time there was dancing we were playing some melody with the

Ward Theatre, built by the Henriques brothers for Col. C. J. Ward (courtesy National Library of Jamica).

wrong rhythm. He was right to complain, but it would have been easier to have seen the film first. I had been leading the pit band at the Palace and at Movies for around three years by the time the regiment broke up in 1926, so it was easy for me to gravitate to the theatres of Kingston. Now the cinemas were open from 6.30 to nearly midnight, with a main feature film, the news, and a special film – which would now be called a documentary. Just imagine – all over the world people were watching the same movies, and pit bands were struggling to add the right music.

In the years when I lived in Jamaica it was quite the thing to be a member of a brotherhood or lodge, such as the Freemasons or the Oddfellows. I played at Masonic functions. Indeed I was asked if I would like to join, but it didn't interest me. Of course such organisations played a great part in the lives of the members, for membership made them join together across racial and cultural lines, and provided a help for funerals, and as a little bank in times of need. There was no particular racial distinction in such groups in Jamaica for the bulk of the people were negroes; and Greeks and Jews and Syrians, and Indians and Chinese, were not numerous enough to form their own groups.

I can't recall pot or ganja smoking. As a rum-producing country I assume that most Jamaicans had drunk rum. As in all societies you had those who took a social drink, those who abstained, and the heavy drinkers or rum-heads. I knew we had tropical diseases, for you would hear of someone dying of this, that, or the other, but there was no radio or television to tell you of it, and newspapers were not readily available amongst the natives. Because the media was so small such things would be kept under the carpet. I can well remember the influenza epidemic after the First World War, because it really hit everybody badly. Otherwise the populace was healthy: disease was present but minimal. In the late 1920s I was invited to the country and I can remember the mosquitoes there. The house was used to it, and at dusk they went round and shut all the windows and doors; but the noise was loud. I don't remember any in Kingston.

Law and order was the responsibility of the police, and up to the rank of sergeant major they were black. These fellows were in the peculiar position of being tools of the Europeans, maintaining law and order for the whites. An extraordinary incident, around 1925, comes to mind. You see, the big four in Jamaica were the governor, the colonial secretary, the chief justice, and the officer commanding the island's forces. They were all English, of course. This Chief Justice was fearless in the execution of his justice, and he told a group of whites – young lads – something that soon passed amongst everyone on the island. Young whites had the upper hand in Jamaica, some of the time, taking advantage of their racial position, abusing the natives. He was hard on them, telling them that the law was there for everyone to obey, and that they – as whites – should set an example. We soon found out about this, and our estimation of the man was high. Years later, in London in the 1930s, I was going to Berwick Street market, and I saw him waiting for his wife. I passed him, and our eyes met (he had a monocle), but I didn't speak, for his face was not inviting. I admired the man, and his stance that a judge must uphold the law in its truest sense. There wasn't a great deal of crime in Jamaica in those days. There were prisons, for thieves and chaps who assaulted others, and so on. Now and then there would be a murder, which was a sensation: 'a Chinaman got killed last night', and everyone would go to have a look at where the poor chap had died. I think it was the same in England at that time, too.

There were labour riots in 1923, in the plantations, but we heard about it at Up Park Camp because some of the regiment

Palace Theatre, Kingston (courtesy National Library of Jamaica)

was sent in to show the flag but I don't think they did anything. At that time there were no British regiments in Jamaica, for they came in around 1925 to replace the WIR which was disbanding. The East Yorkshires and the Green Howards were there then. Jock Howie was in the band of the Green Howards.

There were others of similar high moral standing in high places in colonial Jamaica. Brigadier L. S. Blackden,[5] the Officer Commanding, used to take the Scout parades, and he would speak to the lads. He was tall and lanky, with ginger hair; he used to scratch his bottom as he talked. Uplifting talk, injecting a high moral fibre into Jamaicans. Men like that set a standard for me, lifting me to a higher concept of life. We admired it. Such people, the headmasters, and teachers, and so on, were admired. We knew you had to work at it – the peg was above your reach, so you had to stretch out and up.

After my return from Wembley I was connected with some

young intellectuals. Most of them had some clerical job in the civil service. I was very, very friendly with Edna Lamont, who was a typist to the Mayor of Kingston. Today we would say that she was a secretary. She was a very skilled stenographer, the best in the island, and she should have been the Governor's typist but that job went, of course, to an English girl. The usual reason. The two knew each other – Edna was well respected. She was an enthusiastic pianist and I helped her with her music. She had a sister named Vera, who had been to America. In their home was a small book, *Jamaicans With Backbone*, which listed fellows who were or had been doctors, barristers, members of the legislative council, and so on. They were just names to me but that book influenced me, for it inspired me, and I felt it was important to be a Jamaican with backbone.

Our band sergeant after Beek, and before Eldon Stewart, was George Neilson, who had won the silver medal at Kneller Hall around 1907. He was a cornet player, and he also played the violin, so I worked with him when a string section was needed. Actually the pride of Jamaica was Jacky Lewis, whose violin playing so impressed a visiting composer from England that he dedicated some music to Lewis. Yes, another coloured Jamaican – with backbone. And I must remember Sgt Gravesande, who started a band in Port Antonio or Montego Bay. It was a youth band, in the 1920s. He took on virgin soil, indeed. These chaps – Reid, Knibbs, Neilson, Gravesande – were anxious to use their skills; they were filled with the desire to advance their profession amongst their own people. They had few resources and next to no money, but they struggled to develop Jamaican skills and knowledge of music. Such men had a long influence, over generations of Jamaicans, and could be called patriots as well as professionals.

When Vera Manley – Ludlow Moody's wife, that is – formed her quintet I was the only male, and the only dark one! I played my cello; there was a red-haired English girl whose name escapes me, who played the violin; and a Jewish lady named Mrs Delgado, who taught at one of the better schools, played the viola. Miss Clerk, whose father – or was it an uncle? – owned the music shop on King Street, was another violinist. She was a white Jamaican. And Mrs Moody was a mulatto. So I was bottom of the heap. We were asked to the Governor's house to play at some event, for this Governor's wife was outgoing and she wanted some decent music at their official functions. King's House was more like a palace, really. By the way, the army band had played in the grounds for garden parties. Well, all the guests were European, and there was Vera Manley – Mrs Moody – being introduced to everyone as the leader of the quintet. The Governor's wife made sure I was being seen to but outside, in his car, was dear Dr Moody. I wished that I had a car to go and hide in during the interval. That was the price you had to pay if you aspired towards the highest level in society, Jamaican society, and you weren't white or near white.

I used to go to Ludlow Moody's house to rehearse with the ladies. It was a great big, European-style house, with servants. I didn't have a great deal to talk about with Ludlow, just chat and trivialities. He was placed in this position where, although our skins were the same colour, he was in a set having to be European. And if you aimed you became: so there was a social gap between us. As a medical man he was well publicised, and had a good practice. He had resigned from government service to practise privately. Most of his patients were white; rather, over half were Europeans. His fees were a little high. I went to him a couple of times and the first consultation cost me a guinea – and I was a native! I don't know about outside Kingston, but doctors were white or nearly white, with some darker ones here and there. You really had to have a reputation like Moody to practise successfully if you were coloured.

He had his car; I still had my British bike. After the army band broke up I went to live with Alf Scott. Scott, the trombonist who had gone to Kneller Hall with Callender and Ricketts in 1911, had left the army when I was at Kneller Hall, but we played together on my return. We played cello duets, and I visited his home. So I had digs with him from 1926. He, his wife, her sister, four daughters, and a boy named Jacky. There was Agnes, Nellie who went to America, Cecile who was my god-daughter, and Terri. And one time Alf Scott and I played in the orchestra at the Palace Theatre – which was a cinema. Scott had a large house at Rose Gardens, close to the Palace, which he got for nothing or next to nothing. It was owned by the syndicate which owned the Palace, and he had some caretaker responsibility. Like those of Sgt Gordon, they weren't much. I was getting five to seven pounds a week at

Alf Scott, trombonist and cellist

Marie Scott: Thompson lived with the Scotts from 1926 to 1929.

the Palace as band director and the musicians were getting three or so. The audiences were mixed but there was segregation based on price. The cheaper the seats, the darker the customer. Up in the gallery there were real enthusiasts. At the Ward Theatre, with its stage acts and plays, they would really applaud a good performer. There were stage shows at the Palace, too. The Ward had visiting troupes, playing opera, drama, comedy, that sort of thing. It was at the Ward Theatre in December 1927 that Marcus Garvey spoke after he left America. I'll tell you about Marcus later on. At Ward's I was an instrumentalist, not the band director. I do recall arranging the orchestral parts for Joe Derbyshire, who had studied the piano in America, when he played a concerto. It was at Ward's, a piece by Rubinstein I think. He died of meningitis in the 1920s. I played with him at Movies. Frank Cellier's drama company played there for three or four weeks, with real West End of London performances of serious drama, which were very good.

I remember that another fellow put on a show, based on the Tutenkhamen discoveries in Egypt by Howard Carter in 1922, when all those ancient things were found. This show had an 'Eastern' flavour and exotic dancing, with the girls wearing very little. Peter Kirkaldy organised their show. His day job was being in charge of the stables for the dirt carts of Kingston.

We knew all about America with its segregation and the way they had imprisoned Garvey, and those vigilantes, and lynchings, because it was all reported in our papers. I once saw a photograph of negroes hanging, and the mob around them. That was our knowledge of the southern states so it was New York for Jamaicans. In the 1920s West Indian negroes were just getting into show business in America, with Eubie Blake and Noble Sissle's shows, so some of our musicians went there. Just as Egbert Thompson had made it in New York around

1910, so Wington Thompson and others went off to join Blake in the 1920s. So there I was, playing in the theatres and cinemas of Kingston, living at the Scotts, and playing with Vera Moody's quintet. In mid-1929 Sam Manning came from New York to the Palace, which was a little unusual for most of the acts were white. I was band director at the Palace theatre at the time, May 1929. His song and dance act was quite North American but entertaining. Now the cinema work was ending as talking pictures had come in; they had their own sound, and as cinemas were converted, bands – all over the world – were no longer needed. I had an inflated optimism, and decided to go to England. I recalled Egbert Thompson's success in France, and that news item about Louis Drysdale, and my happy days in England in the army, so I packed up all my instruments, bought a ticket, and left Jamaica for England. In my passport I see that it was issued on 25 June 1929, and that I was a 'British subject by birth'. Profession: musician.

3

My Face is my Fortune

I disembarked at Dover from a banana boat destined for the Continent, then I took a train to London's Victoria station and then a taxi to the address of a family in west London's Fulham.[1] Now, I had worked with Joe Appleton in Jamaica, in the army band, and he had gone absent without leave some years before. He had taken one of those small cargo boats to Cuba, and from there had made his way to Britain. Another soldier who had gone AWOL was trombonist Ralph Russell, who went to the States. Appleton played the saxophone. I think he went off to Cuba in 1924; certainly it was before 1926. I believe he was living in Birmingham – or perhaps Manchester – it was in the Midlands. He knew the family in Fulham and had arranged that I should stay with them when I first arrived in England. It was a coloured family. The father had died. There were, let me see, three daughters and one son. The oldest girl was in her twenties, and I should think that she had made contact with Appleton when he was playing in a dance band. He was a good saxophone player, and coloured fellows were pretty rare, so maybe that's how the contact had been made. Anyway, the next day, on the Sunday, I went right across London by taxi, to digs in Grove Road, off the Mile End Road. It was a theatrical lodging house, and there never was any trouble over race at these places. Can you imagine the variety of people who stayed in the theatrical digs? Chorus girls, musicians, acrobats, clowns, comedians, fellows with snakes, and lord knows what else. So coloured people were not treated badly – only considered different.

Joe Appleton must have told his friends about this place, for how would they know of it? Joe had also given me the address of a bandleader in nearby Dalston, and I went to see him that first week. He was a Jewish violinist by the name of Muzikant. He had four sons, all musicians: a nice, kind family. They worked at Jewish weddings and dances. I got a job that Sunday, playing at the Portman Rooms in Baker Street. There must have been one thousand people there. It was a very formal affair; evening dress, etc. We played from six until two in the morning. A sixteen-piece orchestra, playing away whilst all those people ate, drank, talked and laughed. Background music to the chink of glasses. Muzikant pulled out a selection called *Hebrew Melodies*, which I hadn't seen before, but as I was pretty good at sight-reading I wasn't worried. We came to the trumpet solo; and by the time I was halfway through there was complete silence: no clinking, chatting, or the sounds of knife and fork. There was a thunder of applause at the end of my solo. I got the leader's thumb-up sign (I hadn't seen that before). At the end of that selection he told me that I had played the famous Jewish tune 'Eli, Eli' with great success: all the guests knew and loved it, and my rendition was to every-one's satisfaction. He asked for my diary (that also confused me: I hadn't got one); but wrote down over thirty dates and gave the list to me. Each job or gig as we say in the music busi-ness, would put me in contact with different musicians; they talked about the coloured trumpeter, and so I would get more work. Six weeks or so after my English music career started I had no work.

The Jewish religion has a month of no celebrations, so Muzikant's band rested. That was my first experience of real unemployment. It was a shocking, and frightening, experience, because I was an utter stranger in a strange land and I had nothing to support me. It was 1929, and there was no DHSS government department to step in and help. I looked for work, in factories and offices; I recall following up advertisements, going along to a firm's headquarters, where some flunkey would stop me at the door. Then, having ascertained my reasons for calling, he would go inside. And, over the top of the wood and glass partitions that were common in offices in those days, you would see faces – taking a good look at this coloured fellow. And, of course, there was no vacancy. There was little work for musicians, unless you were specialised. Muzikant had the Jewish wedding scene; otherwise there were hunt balls, and agents supplied groups for such society dances. If you were known to be a reliable fellow then you stood a chance. Mind you, with Muzikant I was paid one pound for gigs which went from six until two in the morning. When I first arrived I thought that a couple of gigs a month would keep me in comfort. How wrong I was.

So, there I was in London, with no work. There were no jobs because of prejudice: it was the same with boarding houses – 'it's not me that is racially prejudiced, but the others mind.' I seldom met any of these 'others'. I got some work in music and other things pulled together, and I survived, but it was a really frightening time for me. I don't actually recall the sequence of how I got out of it. But I did.

One or two times I owed the rent money but the landlady trusted me. I had no regular work, so I told her that I would pay her when I got a gig, and that the next one was in so many days. Once I was so broke that I only had sixpence [2.5p], so I went to Woolworth's where they had a biscuit counter; biscuits came in large tins then, and they were on show with glass lids. Woolworth's was then the 3d and 6d store – nothing cost more than sixpence. At the end of the biscuit selection, where you had your biscuits weighed (there weren't any packets then), there was a tin where they put the broken biscuits. You could buy a pound [450 gm] of broken biscuits for 3d. And that's what I ate. There was no work, outside the entertainment and music business, for black people. Believe me, I tried.

I had realised from London musicians that Archer Street and Charing Cross Road were the places to look for work if you were in the music and entertainment business, for there were the music publishers, arrangers, and theatrical agents. It was slap in the middle of London's theatrical district, and so I meandered up there. I had heard about a show called *Brown Birds*, which was employing coloured artists, and I met Will Garland, the Afro-American manager. I had a talk with him, and he said I was welcome to join the show's orchestra. So I did, for about four weeks, and we toured to Brighton, and Bristol, and a couple of other places. I think that this was early part of 1930 but it may have been late in 1929. Anyway, after this I went back to London, and took digs in Kennington over the river, and worked in the Jewish wedding scene. I well recall playing at one such gig in Holborn, and after it I took the tram down, under Kingsway, and changed at the embankment. I had no overcoat and the first dart of winter struck me as I waited there on the Thames embankment for my tram to Kennington. As I stood there, freezing, I promised myself that I would buy myself an overcoat and a pair of gloves first thing the next morning. And so I did. I went to a secondhand clothes shop and got a 'nigger brown' overcoat, and some gloves. That lasted me until I was in Cochran's shows, when I was paid £25 a week. Actually, with all the rehearsals and practices and so on, that first week with Cochran in Manchester in 1931 got me the then-fantastic sum of £120. It is still a good sum today, fifty years on. And in Manchester I bought a llama overcoat, almost to my ankles. I had that super coat right through the tour with Louis Armstrong in the winter of 1934, and later.

Will Garland was a very experienced American showman, and he ran *Brown Birds*. He sang, and did comedy routines. Evelyn Dove, a contralto, was the lead female singer. I would say that she was born here, from her accent, but they tell me that her father was a wealthy merchant in Sierra Leone, an African businessman. She had been in Paris and all over Europe, as had Will Garland. One of the male dancers was Stanley Coleman, a British lad, a coloured lad. He was a quiet chap, a little effeminate, and I heard that he was badly beaten up during his military service during the 1940s. I think he was from the Midlands, originally. There was a troupe of a dozen coloured girls. One was Lily Jemmott, and she had played with Joe Appleton. She was from Cardiff, and she played the piano, and danced. Years later she married Dr Dele Alakija, who had studied medicine at Guy's Hospital, London. I knew him and his brother – a younger brµother, Tunde. I met Tunde's sister, Aduke, too. There were five sons; their father was well known

Leslie Thompson in llama coat.

in Nigeria, and had a seat on the legislative council there. Tunde played the part of an African prince, not in this show, but in real life. He would impress that certain type of person who loved titles, and we would bump into him in the clubs in London in the 1930s. I never did know what happened to him but, anyway, Lily Jemmott was one of the acts in *Brown Birds*.

Because the show had lots of singing and dancing the orchestra had to be pretty good, and I must say that Micky Summers, the Jewish chap who directed us, was very good. I was the only brown bird in his band. Top of the bill was a duo, a white couple, in evening dress, who danced and sang. It was a good road show, and we got the audiences. There was one scene, with Evelyn Dove with a Mammy's headscarf, and the chorus girls gathered round her. She sang all those Mammy songs – 'Mighty Lak a Rose,' 'Swing Low,' 'I Got a Robe' – that sort of thing. She had a very fine voice. The band was as small as it could be, for the financial restraints were important. I think there were a dozen of us: two violins, piano, trumpet, trombone, drum, that sort of thing. We really had to work, for the show was very musical.

As well as Stanley Coleman, another British coloured lad in that show was Arthur Dibbin, and I knew him for years. He was from Wales, and he was singing in this show. He had a wonderful baritone, a very fine voice. When my black face appeared in the pit orchestra I think he was encouraged to return to the trumpet which he had played in the brass bands of South Wales; so, eventually, he became a trumpet player as well as a singer. We worked together in 1936. It was in 1979, I think, when I was speaking at a church meeting in Tottenham, somewhere in north London, I met his father-in-law, who told me that he had recently died.

It was in the winter of 1929 that I met Dr Brown, who was the first resident coloured person I met in England. I had stiff fingers and told my landlady, who suggested that I ought to go up Grove Road to see the coloured doctor. So I crossed Victoria Park and called on Dr James Jackson Brown in Lauriston Road. Of course he made me most welcome, and told me that my stiff fingers were a result of the cold weather. This must have been around October 1929, I suppose. J. J., as Dr

Brown was called by his friends, was from Jamaica, and had been in London for years. He had married a Jewish lady and they had two boys who were young men when I first met them. Leslie was twenty and Gerald was twenty-three. Milly Brown played the piano, and she had all the sheet music from the shows; I well remember going there with my trumpet and playing duets for an hour or more. I was in top condition, and in good form. I met other chaps at the Browns but I don't recall their names. You know the way it is – meet Leslie, here's so-and-so. Brown knew many people, not just Jamaicans. I must say that I still admire the way the English people remember names so easily. I don't recall any of them at the Browns except Mrs Lou Cambridge. I gave her a lift in my car, so that would have been around 1932. As we drove to the station she kept telling me to be careful, and slow down, and so on. I understand that her husband Alfred Cambridge was from British Guiana, and I knew that the Browns and the Cambridges had been friends since well before the war, twenty years or more. He was a law crammer but had died rather young, before I got to London. At that time, around 1930, I was pretty busy, and as so many of the people I met then I was to know over the years, I can't tell how and when I met each and every one.

Rudolph Dunbar came over from Paris; it must have been a few weeks after I arrived from Kingston. I think he had been in France for some time, but I don't know when he had left [British] Guiana. He was a clarinettist, trained in the police band, and he went on to some fame when his clarinet tutor book was published shortly before the Hitler war. I may have met him through Al Jennings, a fellow from Trinidad who had been in London for some time. Gerald 'Al' Jennings was a guitarist; he lived above a dry cleaning shop in the Edgware Road. He had a wife and a little boy. He was a tailor, but no great shakes as a musician. He wrote a song and got me to harmonise it, but I don't think anything came of it. Now I did know George Clapham at this time: that is to say, at the time I first got to know the Browns in Hackney, and heard about Garland. George was a pianist who had been in London a while, too. He was, I think, also from Trinidad. He had been in London since the early 1920s and, I believe, had worked for the Danish film star Carl Brison. Well, George Clapham thought about forming a coloured band, and he got me, Jennings, and a drummer named Newton – another Trinidadian. Gus Newton had been here for some time, too, for he had a boarding house near Kings Cross station. Perhaps he had been with Clapham in some Trinidad military contingent in the war.

Joe Appleton was involved, too, as was Lily Jemmott; and we had Monty Tyree on saxes, too. I shared digs in Kennington with Monty. He had a brother named Henry, and Harry Tyree toured with Louis Armstrong when I was in that band. They were British-born coloured chaps, from the Birmingham area. I still believe that a good coloured band would have got work in England at that time, and our effort was ambitious – very ambitious. It was an effort. At that time, all the American jazz records were being released in England, and the sounds of Armstrong, Ellington, Lunceford, and all those big bands, were all the fashion. So Clapham had this ambitious scheme, and we rehearsed, and we went to agents, and to theatrical booking fellows, and so on. But I think we sounded like little children against those American bands. Clapham would go in to see this fellow, or that fellow, after our audition and he would come out and tell us that we would be getting a letter, or a phone call, very soon. It was an ambitious failure, but we weren't a good standard and I think those rejections were right. We did get one job, for a week or so, at a dance place in Tottenham; we replaced the regular band which was on holiday.

Al Jennings had been in Britain for years, and his friend Clapham had been involved with the American clarinettist Sidney Bechet. Anyway, Jennings took me out to the Essex county cricket playing fields, by car, where J. J. Brown's West Indian cricket team was playing. I think they were playing a reserve side of Essex, or perhaps it was a friendly. It was the first time I had seen English cricket, so I suppose this was the summer of 1930. Some of those West Indian boys could play, and I heard the Essex team talking about one fielder who was rushing about and catching one fellow here, and fielding brilliantly there, that they would have to watch him when Brown's team went in to bat. He was like greased lightning. That West Indian team was mainly medical and law students and doctors, and old Brown had formed it years before.

It was at the Browns that I mentioned the time I had seen Drysdale's picture in the *Gleaner*, and – of course – they knew Louis Drysdale. So I got his address, and I went over to Westbourne Road in Forest Hill, south London, to meet him. He had been teaching other negro singers in London, but his tuition of Florence Mills around 1923 was his big advertising gambit. His wife was English. His voice coaching school wasn't doing too well, and he worked as a tailor and taught between stitches, as it were. He hired a hall – the Steinway Hall near Regent Street, by the hour. One of his pupils was the wife of Harry Leekam, and Dr Leekam played cricket in Brown's team. He was from Trinidad. He was very Chinese looking, and so was his brother Ferdie Leekam; Harry's medical practice was near Euston, but Ferdie was still studying. When I went to see Leslie Brown in the summer of 1984 – I hadn't seen Leslie for years – he told me that Ferdie Leekam qualified during the war. Gerald Brown went to the London Hospital in the 1930s and he qualified there, just as J. J. had. I last saw Leslie Brown, until my visit last summer, in 1932, at the back of the Adelphi Theatre. I was playing for one of Cochran's shows – *Words and Music* by Noel Coward – and had done the matinee when I returned to my car. It didn't work, and I was looking inside, for inspiration! Leslie Brown came along, and fixed it. He was a trained automobile engineer, and he soon saw that some joker had swopped over the plug leads. He went off to Africa soon after that: I didn't see him again until last summer in Norfolk.

Now there was another fellow, named Oscar Dawkins, around in London when I first settled here. He was a drummer, and probably from the West Indies, but I can't be sure and nobody was sure then, either. He was keen to exploit the concept of an all-coloured band, and I rehearsed with him – and Monty Tyree, Joe Appleton, and the girl pianist Lily Jemmott, and some others. It was quite separate to Al Jennings and Clapham's group. Dawkins was living in either Lambeth or Kennington, and was in his mid-thirties; he was a character. Any rumour that was going had to include Oscar Dawkins' name. He was always in fights: disputes and fist fights. The last I heard of him was when he broke a chair on someone's head in a club in London, sometime in the thirties. And none of us saw him again.

Lily Jemmott (I'm sure it's that, but if Joe Deniz said it was Lily Jemmet perhaps he's right, for both came from Cardiff) was Oscar's pianist. In the West End of London there was a club run by a fellow named Pops. He was in his sixties and was memorable because he had an enormous head, with bushy hair. Lily worked there, as a solo pianist, and Oscar Dawkins had got her the job. She dressed like a man for this job, with an Eton crop, collar and tie, and clothes like a barrister. It was marvellous. I don't know if they knew she was a woman. She passed as a man, for the jacket covered her bosom.

In Jamaica a well known comedy duo was Ernest Cupidon and Horace Ableton, and I well remember Cupidon. Leslie

Brown reminded me that he and his father had been very amused by Cupidon and me doing the two old ladies gossiping over a fence routine, but I don't think that was on stage – probably in that big house J. J. had in South Hackney, where all sorts of people would pop in. I think Cupidon was visiting England, and I suppose he might have toured the theatrical circuit here, but not well-known circuits like the Empire. Perhaps a variety agent had put him on the bill. I had seen him at Ward's, which had coloured shows as well as white. Actually, when the cinema people got organised, shows were put on at the moving picture houses in Kingston as well as at Ward's. Cupidon's act involved funny hats, umbrellas, leaning on the fence, gossiping in dialect: 'Did you hear this one?' He was very popular, for he had a natural and easy wit: a natural genius – no script. I think he was in the civil service in Kingston.

There was a scarcity of coloured people in London, and so we would hear about another fellow, and so the word would get round. Before I tell you about one place where it was easy to mix with coloured fellows, I should tell you that Harold Moody, who was Ludlow's eldest brother, was active in social affairs for West Indian and African people in Britain.[2] He had a good medical practice in south London, and he had various contacts, some of them the same people as J. J. Brown, of course. And there was John Barbour-James who was from Guyana: he had worked in Africa in the 1900s.[3] He lived in west London, and put on very high-class events for other West Indians. I well remember going to one such function at the Northumberland Rooms off Trafalgar Square, run by Barbour-James. It was an evening dress and formal affair. I may well have met Jack London there. He was a pal of Leslie Brown, who told me last year that London lived in Marylebone with an eccentric uncle named Williams. Williams had made some money, back in the 1890s, in Guyana, and he had come to England. He married an

Englishwoman. And Jack – he was really Edward London – lived with them. He found the atmosphere a little oppressive, for he was a young fellow. Old Williams had a mechanical horse, with a motor bike engine, and all the horse-like movements, or so Leslie Brown was telling me. I went there but don't recall the horse at all. Jack was an Olympic runner: he had run for Britain at the Olympic Games, in the relay. Leslie Brown had handled the baton, and I knew, somehow, Jack had been a sprinter. I think it may have been the 1928 Olympic Games, but I don't know. Jack grew to be a good friend of mine.

Jack's father was a doctor in Georgetown, and Jack was in London, and was supposed to be studying medicine, but he dabbled with the piano, and, as there was a demand for coloured artists, he gave up his studies. I might have met Jack at John Payne's place in Regent's Park Road, which had been given to him by the philanthropist Lady Cook. It was a centre for coloured American artists, singers and performers. John Payne had lived there from the 1920s, when he left the Southern Syncopated Orchestra. He knew so many people, like Evelyn Dove, and Paul Robeson. Jack London was his pianist. I worked with Jack London in Cochran's *Cavalcade* in 1931.

As well as these people, like Brown, Moody, London, Payne, Jennings, Drysdale, and Williams, there were layabouts, coloured fellows who were pimps, or occasional sailors, who worked as bouncers in clubs, who were on the fringes of the theatrical world. They met at Trini Mendez's cafe in St Giles' High Street, where Centre Point is at Tottenham Court Road. Mendez was from Trinidad. His cafe, which was nothing to write home about, was a meeting place for coloured people in London before better places like Jig's and the Nest. Some of these layabouts got jobs, as bit-part actors, in a film which was being shot at Welwyn Garden City, and working in that studio was Nigel Hill, known as 'Cod' Hill. So Cod, who played the

Thompson with Jack London in *Cavalcade*. Publicity photo displayed outside the London theatre in 1931 (courtesy Jeffrey Green).

string bass, asked them if they knew of a coloured trumpeter, because he wanted to set up a jazz band and, having heard Louis Armstrong's recordings, thought that you had to be coloured to play like that. So I heard about Cod Hill, and we made contact, meeting at Scarth's shop in Charing Cross Road. I did some odd jobs with Cod, and in the summer of 1930 or 1931 I went with him to Tagg's Island.

A wealthy chap named Bundy owned the island, which was in the Thames west of London; not a big river, there, of course, but the island had a grand hotel built at the beginning of the century and a certain type of person found it to be pleasant. People would motor out there for dinner and a dance; others would stay the night; and some were there for the weekend. It was really for high-class dirty weekends. There were lots of places of that sort, then. Girls from cabarets and shows, and fellows they had met, would go there. I remember being called to one table, where a girl (I had seen her before) was with a

Nigel Finch-Hill's Rhythm-Fish 1930. The leader was only eighteen (courtesy Nigel Hill).

fellow, who told me to always call him sir. I paused, looked at him, and called him sir, because my face was black. If I was disrespectful I would be the first to go through the door. That girl knew the sort of fellow she was with, after that incident. Cod and I, with two others, shared a house nearby that summer of 1931. The Thames Riviera Hotel was a high-class place with a wealthy clientele.

Looking back on that summer of 1931, it was a holiday. Of course I was at work, but we played for three hours a day – with an afternoon tea dance on Sunday – and Monday off. We were advertised in the London papers as either Nigel Finch-Hill and his Music or as Cod Hill and his Rhythm Fish and there were six or seven of us. Harry Weston and Reg Conroy lived at home, and Cod and I shared with Jack Melford and Jack China. We were joined by Cyril Harling with his violin on Saturday nights, but the rest of us doubled. Harry played the saxophone and the clarinet. Reg played both the piano and the trumpet, and Jack sang and played the drums. Jack China played the clarinet and the tenor saxophone, I played the cello, trumpet, trombone, and string bass and Cod played the reeds and the string bass. We used to leave the washing-up for a whole week. We had bicycles and peddled around, and that summer went on and on, or so it seemed.[4] Around this time Louis Armstrong's records were coming into Britain. I had never heard anything of him in Jamaica, but Cod Hill and other fanatics had his records. I can well recall 'West End Blues,' and 'Memories Of You.' Absolutely marvellous – the style was new to me, and that swing, that beat, was tremendous. Everyone was listening to the records, and certainly I had never heard bands with that beat before. Our hotel bands were just milk and water by comparison. That beat and punch, and swing. It taught me a lot, and I knew that my concept of trumpet playing was lacking. Well, as the song title has it, 'My Face Is My Fortune,' and I was the only coloured trumpeter in London when Louis' records became the talk of the music business, and so my face was my fortune. Cod Hill spoke to Spike Hughes, who also was a bass player. Spike's father had been a music critic and Spike had fallen in love with jazz when he was a student, and he had become something of a modern composer. He had a contract to record modern dance music for Decca and he made an effort to contact me. I was in digs off the Hampstead Road in north London, so this might have been in 1930; I really can't recall the events in strict order. Anyway, Spike came along to hear me play all my instruments, and he straightaway pulled me into his group of recording 'angels' – chaps who did regular work and extra work at recording sessions. He had to make four sides a month, that is two records a month. And I became part of that group, working with the best session, orchestra, and dance band musicians in London, from the autumn of 1930. Thanks to Cod Hill and to Spike Hughes.

So, about a year after I arrived in London from Jamaica, I was working with the best musicians. Spike's group never played together outside the studios. We were called the Decca-Dents, a pun of the worst sort. We recorded at the Chenil Galleries in Chelsea, and the rush to the nearest pub (the Six Bells) was immortalised in the band's 'Six Bells Stampede'. We were the first group to play 'three of a kind' – a trombone trio – Lew Davies, myself and a third fellow. That's how Spike built up his reputation, for he tried new ideas. Those records don't sound so adventurous now, but in 1930 and 1931 they had a high reputation. Spike even went to New York in 1933 to record the greatest negro musicians there. He wrote tunes and his arrangements were influenced by Duke Ellington. He composed 'Sirocco' and when we recorded it in February 1932 I was the bass player. Spike normally played the string bass, but he was busy directing the reed section and I picked it up, and played it to give the rhythm section a full sound. When we were ready to record Spike told me to stay on the bass as a full brass section wasn't required. I don't recall if I played the bass on other tunes at that session, but I am sure that I never played the bass with Spike any other time.

Spike's group was a hot band, and he certainly was a good ensemble writer. There were four brass, three saxes, and a four-

Spike Hughes
'Sirocco',
1932.

piece rhythm section. He had advanced ideas and some of them came off beautifully. Constant Lambert, the composer, who was teaching at one of the London schools of music – the Royal College or the Royal Academy – was associated with Spike, and I played for Lambert's *Salome* in the summer of 1931. Lambert made his musical mark with his *Rio Grande* ballet, which was quite something for an Englishman at that particular point. Another avant garde composer of this time was Adolf Busch, and I played with him, too, and one or two others of this circle. Cochran's conductor was Ronnie Greenbaum, who was known to everyone as 'Bumps'. Bumps was an assistant to Sir Thomas Beecham whose symphony orchestra was full of young, brilliant, musicians, really top rate instrumentalists and Bumps was a tremendous conductor, too. He used to look after Beecham's orchestra when the master was elsewhere. Bumps married Sidonie Goossens, who has recently retired from symphonic work. I ran around with this group in the early thirties, for we were all trained musicians and much of an age. The composer William Walton, later Sir William, was in this set, and I can well remember his surprise when I told him that I had arranged his *Belshazzar's Feast* in Jamaica, for George Goode.[5] We hadn't got enough money to buy the complete orchestration, so, unlike Britain, we had to write our arrangements.

Spike got involved with Charles B. Cochran, who was the leading showman of England. He was a theatrical impresario, and promoted shows, boxing matches, and other public entertainments; he had several irons in the fire, with shows touring here and in America, and different shows in different theatres in Britain. He put on shows that had chorus girls – Cochran's 'Young Ladies' – and the format of the shows changed as weeks went by, so you could go to see them more than once and it would have the best of what you had seen, plus novelties. Cochran and Spike were working on the *1931 Revue* and, through his American contacts, got hold of Clarence 'Buddy' Bradley. Buddy was an American negro dancer and choreographer, and I think he had taught Fred Astaire and others more than a trick or two. And he came to England for Cochran, for he was big in Hollywood – as big as you could get with that colour skin. Spike was to write some arrangements for this large orchestra under Percival Mackey, a symphonic dance orchestra, in fact. Spike told me about it and I got the job as first trumpeter. I never looked back, and I was in Cochran's organisation until I decided to make a move away.

Joey and Eddie, the American dancers, were in the *1931 Revue*, and they, just like the coloured American woman dancer who was in *Words and Music* in 1932, brought over the latest hot records from New York. All these Americans had portable record players: that woman in *Words and Music* had coloured dressers too, probably relatives, and they all had the latest records, and we could hear them any time we wanted to. Buddy's boss was Billy Pearce, who had Buddy under contract, but the pair split, due to the opportunities Buddy had seen when first working with Cochran in England. Buddy set up a dance studio in Compton Street, and worked for films and West End shows. He changed the whole style of dancing in Britain. Before Buddy Bradley there were 'hoofers,' which was very much tap dancing. Buddy Bradley introduced movement, and new aspects of dance. There was no change in the music – it was not difficult for us to play. Bradley revolutionised choreography.

Because I worked for Cochran I toured and, when I was in London after the provincial tours, I got back with Spike for the Decca recordings. Some of those contacts I had made, such as the Browns, got weaker. Mind you, students like Alakija were quite separate to the layabouts and fringe people at Trini's cafe. I mixed on the edges of all groups. I also worked in films. Cod

Hill had originally been a trainee technician in that industry, and he had the contacts. I did one film, *A Night In . . .* something or other, in Elstree, before 1932. That involved James Boucher[6] and 'Captain' Harrison who never got the acclaim of Robeson or Norris Smith.[7] Jim Boucher was a tall, light-skinned fellow who had worked in Paris for some years before he came to England in 1930, when we made this film. He was a fine violinist, and he could play the clarinet, and altogether he was a high-powered chap. He was tall and good looking, and projected himself well. He was of mixed parentage but I never met anyone who knew him or anything about him, although I think Arthur Briggs would know about him. He was in his thirties when I met him. He had an aggressive manner, in a way. I would not be surprised to find that he was born in England. He could play jazz, hot dance music, and classics, but I think he went back to France after we made the film, and I haven't heard his name mentioned for years. That film had us in the background, setting the scene, as it were.

I also worked with Hatch and Carpenter. Ike Hatch was a lovely fellow, but he had little proper training, and so his talent was never exploited to the full. I knew him quite well. His voice was pleasant, and he often sang *I Pagliacci* – 'Vesti la giubba.' He did that 'Howsa' stuff, too; no one else was doing it in the thirties. If only these fellows had done their homework, like old Drysdale had done. Get the basis, and build on that. Ike Hatch was successful for some time and was still working in the 1950s, but he was a victim of changes. Just think of the huge talent of Paul Robeson, and the awe which greeted Robeson's singing. He had studied and knew exactly what he was doing. Robeson had been in London since 1928, when he came with Norris Smith and others in *Show Boat*. I hate to say it, but the worst musicians I have worked with have included an overlarge share of coloured ones.[8] I'm not talking about style or the nature of the performer, but the performance itself. Leslie Hutchinson, known as 'Hutch,' the pianist and singer from Grenada, had done his work and he was very popular. His records were sold in the West Indies, I believe, and he had an upper-crust audience. He worked on the liner *Queen Mary*. Mind you, Jack London also had a lot of contacts in high society, as it was called in those days, and I played with him in Belgravia and those rich areas. Fellows like John Payne, and Louis Drysdale, had paved the way. The most exclusive place was Ciro's. Edward, Prince of Wales, used to go there. I went there to see Noble Sissle,[9] and I remember that Sissle had a gold cigarette case which the Prince had given him.

So I was Cochran's number one trumpet in the *1931 Revue*, and from there I was in *Cavalcade*. Four hundred actors and musicians: the orchestra had to be big enough to have a military band on the stage for the Boer War scene. It was Noel Coward's pageant of English life, and it was a tremendous success. I had two stage parts in it, one with Jack London at the piano and Binnie Barnes singing 'Twentieth Century Blues' in a nightclub scene. That picture, which was outside the theatre, also shows one of the actors, whose uncle, I think it was, was Balfour, the old prime minister. You can see the resemblance, I think. And I was also in the ending 'Chaos' scene, when I played the straight Aida trumpet. Some years ago I was having some medical treatment and the doctor recalled that scene – he was a student back in 1931. *Cavalcade* was a mighty hit, so with that and Spike's recordings I was getting regular money.

Those theatre orchestras were capable of playing symphonic music. Indeed, I understand even Sir John Barbirolli had worked in theatre bands. It was not unusual for symphonic musicians to work in theatre pit bands. We had all done our basic training and had mastered our instruments. One time I worked with a chap who had been a professor at Kneller Hall when I was there, back in 1919. And there was Jim Verity from Jamaica, whose mother had been Jacky Lewis' partner. I had been trained correctly at Kneller Hall, and just as I respected my colleagues for their skills, they respected mine. Dunbar tried to get into *Cavalcade*, and sent Elsie Edwards his record of Debussy's clarinet piece, but the orchestra had been fixed by the time he applied. Contracts had been signed and rehearsals had started. I did work with Dunbar in some college dances, those midsummer balls – coloured bands were in fashion. Dunbar was a very smart man, and he had a style that was like the Prince of Wales, and you know how smart he was. Dunbar would put on his evening dress clothes if he was looking for fresh lodgings in the evening! And he had his name in gold on his wrist, so big that you could see it before you could see him. I called Dunbar 'the professor,' by the way, for he was no jazz musician, but a formal, classical player. He had worked for Noble Sissle in Paris, I think.

Then there was Noel Coward's *Words and Music* in 1932, which Spike and Bumps orchestrated. Reginald Burston, who had conducted *Cavalcade*, was the conductor at first, Spike Hughes played the bass and did arrangements. We opened in Manchester in July; by the time we got to London in September 1932 Bumps was the conductor – at the Adelphi. That's when I had Leslie Brown's technical assistance! And there was Noel Coward's 'Mad Dogs and Englishmen' masterpiece in this show. Another Coward song, 'Half-Caste Woman,' from an earlier show, was about a Eurasian woman. Robert Russell Bennett did Jerome Kern's orchestration for *Music in the Air*, which came from New York around 1934. Cochran put it on, and so I was in the pit band at His Majesty's Theatre. Bennett conducted at the dress rehearsal and Bumps listened. On opening night I well recall Bumps looked as if he had had a couple of drinks. He went to his place, and closed his copy. He started the orchestra, and I thought 'What's happening?' and expected a disaster. Bumps was such a superb musician that he had mastered the score and conducted as if it was inside him, from memory. Absolute perfection. No wonder Tommy Beecham had made Bumps his protegee. I went to Spike's place for tea, more than once, and Bumps and Sidonie were there. I also met Frederick Ashton [later Sir Frederick] there, I think. Certainly I remember admiring his artistry, for he really rehearsed that ballet group of his. Buddy Bradley and Ashton got on well together, and they used our Decca record of 'Sirocco' for Ashton's *High Yellow*. This was at the Savoy, with Bumps and members of the London Symphony Orchestra in June 1932 – Freddie Ashton, Alicia Markova, Vanessa Bell – all solidly respectable figures in Britain's artistic world of the 1930s, and later.

I think it was in Coward's *Follow the Sun*, which Cochran put on at the Adelphi, that I spoke to William Walton. That show had Sarah Churchill making her debut, dancing to Walton's *Façade*, which Freddie Ashton had choreographed. Bumps was the conductor, and in the interval of one of our rehearsals I spoke to Walton and told him that I'd arranged his *Belshazzar's Feast* for George Goode in Jamaica. That must have been between 1926 and 1929, between the end of my army days and my departure for England. You may question this as the reference books say that the premiere was in Leeds in 1931, but we did it in Jamaica earlier. It had been reported in the *Musical Times*, and the singers' part was published. I mean, the words and the music. Out in Jamaica we couldn't afford the orchestrations, so George Goode and, I think, another fellow, got me to arrange the orchestral part. It was for a choir in a church, not at Ward's.

Noel Coward knew me, as a coloured member of Cochran's orchestra, and he always spotted me – my face was asking for it. And he would nod. William Walton, I saw a few times; I recall speaking to him and if it wasn't in *Follow the Sun* it was when I was playing in *Words and Music*.

In July 1932 Louis Armstrong came to Britain and I went to hear him. I think every musician in London who could get to the first show at the Palladium was there. Later on I met him. He hadn't got a regular group, so Billy Mason gathered some fellows into a 'hot' band, but they were not regulars, for these chaps had their own bookings and were not always at liberty to play with Louis. It was a very ad hoc affair. Louis rehearsed that band. I remember going to the Palladium with Cod Hill, to hear them going through the routines. Louis' records were available on Parlophone and everyone had them. American coloured entertainers brought others which were not available in Britain, as well as those by Ellington and the other stars. Ellington brought his band to England in June 1933, and they were a wonderful success. Dunbar got to know them, and so did I. Duke gave me a photograph, signed 'To Leslie Thompson – C. B. Cochran's 1st Trumpeter: Best Wishes Duke Ellington.' I was with them one night in Brighton when they had to play a late gig. Time was so short that I drove too fast and the police stopped me. They saw that my car was full of coloured fellows, so they let me go but I was fined ten shillings [50p]. If they had taken me to the police station they would have held three or more of Duke's musicians as witnesses! Duke was a shrewd man, and he had reasoned with his own men. Those who want-ed to make music the way Duke wanted to were happy and stayed with him for years. If they didn't like that music and did-n't care for the hard work that would get those results, they were soon out of the band.

Louis had gone back to New York in November 1932 but he returned to England in August 1933, shortly after Ellington's first visit. He played the Holborn Empire, toured, and then went to Scandinavia. He was back in London at the beginning of 1934. He took a holiday, and his manager went off. Louis hadn't got a band with him, just fellows who had been recruited from Paris by Peter Du Congé. They were mainly Americans, coloured Americans, but there were one or two from Latin America. The pianist was Baretto whose brother was to work with me around 1939. Charlie Johnson was the first trumpet, but he saw the tour as a flash in the pan, and went back to earning his bread and butter in Paris. Before I tell you how I joined Louis I should tell you something of the troubles there could be in running coloured bands.

One of the West India Regiment musicians, a trumpet player named 'Manny' Smith, had settled in Holland and somehow had got to know the Ciro's Club management in London. He was asked to get a good coloured group, and Manny wrote off to Wington Thompson in New York. Wington and another regimental musician from Jamaica, whose name was Wallace, somehow revived the British passports which they had when they left Jamaica in the early 1920s, and this meant they had no work permit troubles in Britain. Gus Newton, Smith, Wallace, Thompson, and a fine American violinist named Leon Abbey (I'm sure that Joe Appleton had told me of Leon Abbey, who had played in London in the late twenties) were rehearsing for the prestigious Ciro's Club venture in the spring of 1933 when the police arrested Wallace and Thompson. A third Jamaican soldier-musician, in New York, really wanted to get to London, and Manny had refused to make him an offer, so he told the American authorities that the pair had revived their old, British, citizenship, and this had been passed to London. So the British police told the now-American saxophone section to get out, and poor old Manny had no band. He went back to Holland and as far as I know remained on the Continent.

I joined Louis, travelling to France via Dieppe where my passport was stamped on 22 October 1934. I left Dieppe on

4 November, returning on 6 November, and then we were on the road. We had rehearsed in Paris, and made some records[10] – 'Tiger Rag' and 'St Louis Blues'. We did a concert, and then – 'Louis Armstrong et Son Orchestre Formidable' on the side of the coach – we went to Switzerland. We were in Italy in January 1935. We played Turin, Marseille, and Paris. Every place was sold out, such was his fame. I used to worry about fires because the halls and theatres were so packed. We had to autograph programmes for the fans, so it was a lot of hard work. Louis had been playing his show tunes for years, wearing them like sand and sea wears a rock, and they were reduced to beautiful, simple, and romantic masterpieces. Every tune had been perfected in this way and you could hear him play the same thing every time. It was always his conception of the melody. Years later I heard him in London and he was playing the same, beautiful, way.

We had no programme in a formal sense, for Louis felt what the audience was like, and played to them. He was an

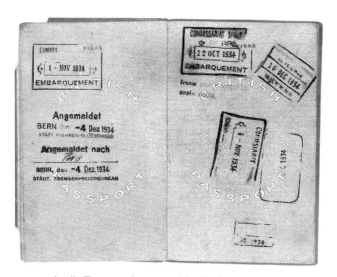

Leslie Thompson's passport for the Armstrong tour

Leslie Thompson and friends, Marseille, 1934, during Armstrong's tour of France

entertainer, but he was not doing the clowning he did in later years. He used to stomp round the stage and he was full of energy, so his personality had the same fire as his trumpet playing. After the performance we went off, and in clubs and late spots he would be asked to play. He didn't; the promoter had paid him, so why give it away. He gave every encouragement to local musicians, especially the youngsters. I usually shared with Harry Tyree, whose brother I had first met through Al Jennings and George Clapham in my early weeks in London, but sometimes it was with another saxophone player, Cass McCord, who was an American. He had been in London in *Blackbirds of 1934*. There was a break of a week or two around Christmas and I joined Leon Abbey, playing at the Hague in Holland; I rejoined Louis in Italy and the tour finished, with a handshake, in France. It was terrific, but I had to get back to London and start again.

I have to say that there were only two jazz musicians, apart from Louis, in that band: Cass McCord and pianist Herman Chittison. Charlie Johnson had worked with Jack Hamilton, who was a Latin American fellow who spoke Spanish. Later on, the trumpeter was Arthur Briggs, whose mother was from Barbados, which is why I thought he was West Indian, not American. He had been in Europe since the days of the Syncopated Orchestra in 1919. During the tour I got to know these fellows, and Louis, quite well. I heard that Collins, the old manager, had booked six weeks back in the summer of 1933 and then had left for the USA, leaving Louis to get a new schedule. When he started asking around he was told that the old rate, of £1,000 a week, was not available anymore as he wasn't the novelty attraction he had been just some days before. That really broke it between Louis and Collins, for Collins had been giving Louis £250 (which had to pay for the band, too) and keeping the rest. It was during his 1933 tour that Louis' lip caved out. He was doing too much work, demanding too much of his lip. If you have any flaw in the skin of your lips you have to nurse it, but Louis didn't and he paid the price.

To tell you the honest truth you could tell he was a trumpet player who had taught himself to play from the way he warmed up. Those phrases were quite different to the warm up phrases of the trained player. You can tell a schooled player. Louis' music was alien to orthodox music: he was in a class by himself. I doubt if training would have changed him, either then or way back when he was in New Orleans. His own musical concept developed undiminished. So it would had he had classical-style tuition. His style suited him; and his tutors or coaches would have tried to cut off half his ideas. But he was like a comet in the sky. His genius, and his means of producing what he did, were simply his very own way. His capabilities were so phenomenal that he stood and stands alone.

Cass McCord had spontaneity, and his solos were good. On the Paris records our saxophone players were Peter Du Congé, and an American named Alfred Pratt, one of those coloured

Americans in Paris. Peter Du Congé's wife was Bricktop – she ran a very famous club in Paris, and she was a terrific, vital, personality. There was another club in Paris run by Frisco Bingham, and he was in London, in his own club, in the late 1930s. Bricktop was an institution. Anyway, Cass and Herman were brilliant improvisers, whereas the rest of us were readers. I was a paper man; Charlie Johnson and the others could read, but they were used to jazz arrangements and so I doubt if they could have read symphonic works. That jazz music is of a mould; jazz players had a style, so reading was a matter of habit.

In 1934, between shows with Cochran and before I toured with Louis, I was working in a dance orchestra in a Mayfair club. Apart from me it was white. I saw a trombone player, who had some influence in the Musicians' Union, go into the office and spend some time with the boss. He came back a second time, and a third time, and on that occasion the orchestra leader was called into the office. When he came out his face was like a beetroot. When the performance was over he came to me and said that the union had been trying to get an increase in wages, but, as the boss convinced them that he just couldn't pay any more, the trombonist fellow (who was no star player, which might explain why he busied himself in the Musicians' Union) said that he should sack one of the band and distribute that fellow's money to the others. It was, more or less, an order to sack me: I assume that the fellow said 'You can sack the black one.' And I was the first trumpet, too.

I well remember that Friday night, for I walked outside with the union fellow: and thanked him for his loyalty to members of his union. I never ever paid union dues after that but the Musicians' Union never prevented me working in the West End. I'd got that job in Berkeley Square through a drummer named Harry Francis, who worked at the union, which meant that he was in a position to get a band together anytime the

phone rang and someone asked for a band. Finding out about
gigs in that way gave him an advantage. He often phoned me
with offers of gigs and, when there was no theatrical work, I
took up as many of them as I could. That Mayfair job was very
pleasant for those few weeks. You know that nobody said anything to me, right up to 1954, when I left the profession. Not a
word from the Musicians' Union ever.

One of the negro musicians who had recorded for Spike in
New York was Coleman Hawkins, and he was over in London
in 1934 before I joined Louis. I never heard him play but I saw
him after work at the Nest Club in Carnaby Street. He didn't
play there, for he was strictly a businessman. He was managed
by Jack Hylton, and Hylton's orchestra had two first-class
trumpeters: George Swift, who was from Canada, and Philippe
Brun from France. Jack Hylton arranged Coleman Hawkins'
tour, and there were rumours that the tenor sax giant would
meet Louis, but for some reason Louis did not appear. I never
bothered to find out why, but I think that Armstrong was
aware that he was a magnet, a star, and was feted, talked about,
and was an entertainer – playing, and singing, and 'muggin'
lightly.' So why should he share the bill with Hawkins, a mere
instrumentalist? Armstrong was the complete artist.

So, after Christmas, working with Leon Abbey in Holland,
and a time with Louis in Italy and France, I was back in London
in early 1935. There I joined the *Blackbirds* show. I had seen the
Blackbirds of 1934 show in London, and knew George Winfield,
the trumpeter. Actually Cass McCord had been in that group
before he joined us in France. A couple of others left and I still
don't know who I replaced in the trumpet section. We had
three: Clifton 'Pike' Davis, George Winfield, and me. Our
drummer was Alfie Craig, a light-skinned Englishman whose
father was American. I did the *Blackbirds* show at the Coliseum
in London, and toured from March 1935 until the show closed

in May. I recall Pierre de Caillaux, a half-caste, who was our conductor. I don't know much about him; he was an American.[11] He was alright but was no Toscanini!

After I joined the *Blackbirds* at the Coliseum we went to Manchester. The whole group went by train on the Sunday, the usual arrangement, with a carriage reserved for all of us. I was the only non-American negro. To travel with them was so foreign that I felt glad, in a sense, that no whites, no English people, were seeing it all, for the behaviour of the Americans was so inconsistent with English customs. Only a few weeks before, on the Armstrong tour, there were fellows from Puerto Rico, the USA, and Tyree from England. But it wasn't like that on the train to Manchester. The difference between the West Indian and the American was very marked, and aspects of their lives were very foreign.

By this time I knew Hutch [Leslie Hutchinson] – he was very English. His signature tune was 'A Nightingale Sang in Berkeley Square'. In early 1935 the Shim Sham Club opened at the Gerard Street end of Wardour Street, and was fronted by Ike Hatch. He had been in England for some years, as part of the Hatch and Carpenter duo. Well, a Polish Jew named Jack Isow put up the money – he was a very tough fellow. Eventually he had a fight with Ike and there was a court case and damages were paid. Isow hadn't been paying Ike Hatch, it seems. Eventually Norris Smith was the host, but Norris asked Isow for payment in advance so there wasn't the difficulty that Ike had on that score. Ike Hatch was very well-liked in theatrical circles and he attracted some customers in that way. The band was led by Cyril Blake. Blake was from Trinidad, and he had been something on the Paris scene when Egbert Thompson got him to change from guitar to trumpet. He was no great shakes as a trumpeter, but he could play. Whenever I went into the Shim Sham Club different faces were on the bandstand. Blake, and his drummer brother, 'Happy' Blake, had been playing in London clubs for some time.

I was living in a leased house in Marchmont Street, in Bloomsbury. I had the whole house, and I stayed there with my wife – I'll tell you about my wife and the family another time – from 1932 until 1938 or 1939. Once we had a musician guest, a Latin American player – a coloured player, trumpeter – from Cuba, who was here with his daughter. They worked in Cochran's shows. He couldn't get suitable accommodation because of the colour bar. It's a funny thing, but the difficulty in getting accommodation, which was written about by Dunbar in the American press, and experienced by Louis and his band, was due to the closed mind of the natives here. 'My home is my castle', but those British who had travelled, or knew people from abroad, were quite different. The general British person had no objection to us but we didn't enter into their lives. It

Happy Blake and his Boys at the Cuba Club, London, ca. 1935: Happy Blake (dms), Bruce Vanderpoye (bs), Robert Mumford-Taylor (sax), Yorke de Souza (p), Louis Stephenson (sax), Cyril Blake (t), Joe Deniz (g) (courtesy Joe Deniz).

was the same at work. They had close links with certain friends or relatives, and everybody else was excluded. Some of the coloured lads would make friends at Trini's, and later in the clubs, such as the Nest, and the Shim Sham, and Jig's; and there were the Rhythm Clubs, sort of jazz clubs, and there people were more friendly towards you. But you seldom got invited into a British home. My home is my castle, indeed.

In the 1930s I was a Catholic, and I went to church occasionally. There were so few coloured people in England, in church, that colour prejudice was never practised. As for the newspapers, the media in Europe have always presented a picture of coloured people that was their own conception. In the 1930s the race business that is current today was not important; in fact, it didn't arise at all. You might meet the odd individual but most Britons were polite, or interested because you were black. It all changed with the influx of immigrants after the war.

The music I played in *Blackbirds* was similar to that I had played in Cochran's shows. The difference was that it had a marked American flavour. I would even go so far as to say that the Cochran boys could play anything that was placed before them, but they had less musical individuality. Now the American arrangements called for solos, and there the American musicians like Cass McCord really showed their style and ability. I remember a girl doing a belly dance to the 'Black and Tan Fantasy' of Duke Ellington. Pike Davis played first trumpet and George Winfield played a terrific hot solo. You would never have heard that in Cochran's shows. English arrangers didn't do that; they didn't allow the freedom. Americans have a way of writing, a hallmark – like Glenn Miller, it is arranged in a certain way which is distinctive to an individual band.

Although there were lots of problems with work permits, there were so many visiting Americans that it's difficult to recall them all. I recall Norman Thomas [a black American entertainer] in 1930; he had a theatrical act in London but, as I was probably playing elsewhere, I didn't hear them. I went to Ciro's in 1930 or 1931 to listen to Noble Sissle. Was Arthur Briggs with him then? I met Noble – a great worker, with a fantastic repertoire. He had over a hundred songs. A very nice, light voice. We didn't have a lot to talk about, apart from the trivialities. It's interesting to consider attitudes. The Americans were not surprised to find me in London, but they were curious to meet a fellow who belonged to them. So they waited to see – to get their first impressions. They were struck by the fact that I didn't talk American. A black Englishman – it made a difference, so our contacts were usually on the surface. It was different on the Armstrong tour; for I got to know the boys and they got to know me. They were lacking a nationalistic racial pride. They were quite humble and accepted me as a brother. It was due to the fact that we had no great ideas about ourselves. We were not striving; the Americans came from the ghetto, and they would have fitted in back in Jamaica. When you get out of the ghetto you strive by the standards of the society outside the ghetto. The Armstrong bus was a little Harlem. The important thing was that we were the same colour. It wasn't, the first time we met, but on the tour it became important and stayed there. One or two of the boys slipped off to the red lamps; generally we were on the move and seldom had any contacts with local people. It is in the static jobs that you can make outside contacts – and have more chance to stray.

On the subject of sexual liberation, as it could be called today, certain incidents stick in my mind. Leslie Hutchinson, the pianist and singer, was very popular with the high society ladies, and even when he was travelling between jobs there were people who would tell him their telephone numbers – for the next time he was in that town. There were lots of rumours about society people. I don't know if their morals were questionable; it seems their actions were. Robeson's name got tied up with them, and so did Nehru. Ciro's was owned by Countess Mountbatten; I played there when the present Queen was Princess Elizabeth. Well, as Mountbatten was a relative of the royal family, Ciro's became the place to dance, so the titled aristocrats thought. Ciro's was exclusive, whereas Jig's in Wardour Street, the Nest in Carnaby Street, and so on, were not exclusive but they were expensive.

I didn't play at those places, but after my theatrical work was over, and if I was in the mood, I would pop in and see who was in town. In that way I met Norris Smith, Sam Manning (who was over in 1935), and American jazz musicians like Eddie South (the violinist), pianists Garland Wilson and Art Tatum, also Gene Rodgers of the novelty duo (a stage act with an American flavour) and others. These fellows would play when the band at these clubs took a break – sitting in with the band, too. I knew Benny Carter, who came to write arrangements for Henry Hall's radio band, and he asked me to join his group, touring Holland, but I had seen the problems of getting back into the London scene after my Armstrong tour, so I turned him down. I saw Nyas Berry and his wife, the trumpeter Valaida Snow; Alberta Hunter; the composer Spencer Williams; Fats Waller; Bessie Dudley; and Edith Wilson. In my theatre work, in the clubs, or at John Payne's, I met those wonderful artists. Once I was playing in the pit band when Josephine Baker, the toast of Paris, sat in the second or third row of the stalls, and she made me feel as important as the star of the show. She was race conscious. She had been in Paris, with Spencer Williams, back in the twenties.

It's interesting that one of Josephine Baker's biographers wrote that Frisco Bingham was a Jamaican. He wasn't very American, and there wasn't very much of America about him. He could have been a West Indian of some sort. His club, after he left Paris, was in Dean Street. It was really run by a girl named Lydia. What was her surname? Lydia had been one of those coloured dancers in Garland's *Brown Birds*. She was born here in Britain, what they called a half-caste. She didn't do what a lot of women do when they have power – she didn't boss you about. She had the authority but was nice to everybody. But that was in the late 1930s.

The summer of 1935 I worked with Billy Merrin's band, doing the summer season at Ramsgate. He was very popular, and was known as the 'King of the Midlands'. Ramsgate was a very popular seaside resort and we got the job because we could do concerts, theatre work and show band routines. Cod Hill will confirm that I arranged Merrin's signature tune. I played and recorded with Merrin. I was a multi-instrumentalist but

Summer season in Ramsgate, 1935. *Back row, from left*: Wally Talbot (t), Nigel 'Cod' Hill (bs), Leslie Thompson (1st trumpet, arranger), Norman Barker (reeds), Pat Hyde (vcls and accordion), Billy Merrin (ldr, songwriter, arranger).

not having much time to practise my multiplicity, I was a trumpeter now. I made a lot of records over the years for Decca and other companies but it was all in a day's work for me. I could do those gigs in the morning, play a matinee, do an evening show, and visit the clubs just as they were getting going.

I haven't told you how these clubs functioned. Members joined and ordered a bottle for their next visit. It would be arranged with a local wine shop that bottles with the member's name on would be kept there, so when you called at the club the waitor would call the shop for your order. So they qualified as bottle parties, and got round the laws on drinking clubs and so on. A liquor licence wasn't necessary. It was the era of the clubs, with Kate Meyrick and Sgt Goddard and other scandals.[12] All that sort of nonsense. I just walked in – never paid membership, as I was a musician. All sorts of people would be there – nightbirds in the main. The jolly drinking crowd, with 'disturbed' people who couldn't sleep and so sought company; gay people – 'queers' as they were then called (they would take a good look at you; you knew the type); and visitors from the provinces, visiting a show, and seeing the night life, brought in by London friends. Quite a mixture of people.

It was in 1936 I think – it is difficult to remember every date – that I started on the idea of a coloured swing band. I had seen that Dawkins, Jennings and Clapham had the idea back in 1929 and I had played American arrangements with Davis and Winfield, and there were all those records of Afro-American musicians, so I thought that now the time was right. You know there was a peak of negro success in London in the 1930s – Robeson, of course, with those films and on stage, and that magnificent voice, and Nancy Cunard had published *Negro*. I used to see her and her boyfriend Henry Crowder in the clubs, you know.[13] Some more Jamaicans had come to England: Bertie King (he'd been at Alpha); Louis Stephenson and 'Jiver'

Hutchinson, who had been in the regiment with me, and had been at Wembley in 1924; and a pianist named Yorke de Souza. Blake and his brother had decided to enlarge the band scene in London, and had encouraged them to leave Jamaica, but I didn't know that. So I got them working in rehearsals ready to go out on the road and then find a decent club to play in back in London.

The band idea came from Ken Johnson, who was studying languages at High Wycombe,[14] and used to come to my place. I gave him food and took a liking to him. Somehow he had got to America, and there he had seen all the bands, and got the idea to dance to a band. He was from British Guiana, and his father was paying for his education which he was ignoring – taking lessons from Buddy Bradley. I was with Cochran or Merrin. Anyway, I said I would pull a coloured band together. I spent some weeks with them, and realised if it was to survive I would have to lead it, and so I left Cochran. We did

Ken Johnson and
his Swing Band,
London, ca. 1936

well over a month of rehearsing. No, nearly two months. I remember Louis Stephenson saying 'You're a hard man to please.' Eventually white boys would pop in to the rehearsal room, surprised at the sound we were getting. They thought it was an American band! I used the arrangements of Brons,[15] all American: we had them all, so we got an American sound which British bands then lacked. We went on tour, playing the circuit; you signed on and toured cinemas, playing on stage before the main feature film. We would give free performances at hospitals for charity and get local publicity. We had Ken Johnson out front – he was a tall, lean fellow, and he could dance. Abe 'Pops' Clare was on the string bass. He was from the West Indies, and had been in England for years, and lived down near Gravesend. Yorke de Souza played the piano and we had two English boys on trombones: Reg Amore and Freddie Greenslade. They were army musicians, and they blacked up for our shows. Arthur Dibbin was now playing the trumpet (we'd worked for Will Garland, of course), and Leslie 'Jiver' Hutchinson from the WIR band played the trumpet, too. Winnie Cooper, who was British-born, was our vocalist. Louis Stephenson played the saxophone, and so did Bertie King: both were from Jamaica. Bob Taylor – he liked to be called Robert Mumford-Taylor, for he was a well-educated fellow from London – played the saxophone, too. I think his father was from West Africa; Mumford-Taylor is in the car business in north London these days, I believe. Tom Wilson, the drummer, was another British coloured lad. He turned up in 1935. He was in the early stages of learning his craft, but he could play. Joe Deniz, one of three brothers from Cardiff, played the guitar with us.

With all these fellows it might seem odd that we got on so well – African, Welsh, Jamaican, Londoners – and Tom from Birmingham, I think – but in Britain you are black or you are white. And we weren't white. We all expected different treatment, and that united us, as it were. Today it is breaking down, but in those days it was different.

The British idea that coloured people have got rhythm and that nonsense, is really stupid. My band had such a strange rhythm section: Joe Deniz was Welsh; Yorke de Souza was Jamaican, a good pianist but I didn't know him from my time in Kingston; Bruce Vanderpoye was from South Africa; and Tom Wilson was English. I made them rehearse to get that lift that Jimmie Lunceford and Ellington were getting on their records. The brass and reed sections sat and waited as I got the four to work on that rhythm, to get the lift or swing. Not just four beats in a bar, but giving it that American bounce. What they called swing. It was hard work.

There were trombone players, like Alf Scott, in Jamaica, but for some reason none of them had come to England, and we used whites. There was a coloured trombonist in London, a chap named Frank Williams, not the Frank Williams of Trinidad,[16] but born here. He was a little lighter than Joe Deniz. He was very, very, very English, I had met him in London around 1931, at a party. We were the only two black people there, and so we talked. He looked up to me, as a working coloured musician, for Frank had played the trombone in a local band around Poplar. He had a fine tone, and was a lovely player. He was not a jazz player at all. I would say he was around twenty-three or twenty-five when I met him, so he would have been born between 1906 and 1910. He was a Londoner, and had sisters; he was a very home loving boy and he didn't mix, he was so very English. I don't think he was comfortable with West Indians, you see, and his home was so pleasant that he didn't want to go on tour. And if you don't tour you don't get the work, because it was the pattern to bring shows to London after a provincial tour, which gave the show, the dancers, the

band, the actors, the stagehands, and all the team, as it were, a
chance to pull together.

We toured for weeks if not months, and the band was really quite good, although it lacked the individual skills of
American bands. Bertie King I would place close to Coleman
Hawkins as a tenor saxophone player; apart from him nobody
had that American spontaneity essential to good jazz. Well, our
agents said that we should consider settling in at a club, and
two or three weeks later Ken Johnson said that we had a contract, or the chance of a contract, at the Old Florida Club in
Mayfair. The Canadian band of Teddy Joyce was there. The
management had not heard us at all. I knew that we had been
playing together so long that we didn't need the sheet music all
the time. The club's manager was a retired army officer, and
this Captain Halsey asked us to play one afternoon. I told the
lads to keep it quiet as we didn't have to blast out, for we
weren't in a theatre, playing to a thousand or more, but in a
small club. It had a low roof, too. We started with 'Harlem', a
tune by Eddie Caroll, a pianist with Spike. It was all the rage
then. We were much too loud, and Halsey kept stepping back,
until he had reached the far wall. He came back when the number was over, and said 'That's absolutely marvellous – just what
we need.' And so we were in. It was late 1936. Certainly it was
New Year's Eve.

I gave the drummer a tubular bell and said don't knock thirteen tonight. About fifteen minutes before midnight we did all
the old tunes – 'The More We Are Together', that sort of thing,
and then rang twelve, and we played favourites for twenty minutes. At the end everyone was too hot to dance, and we had to
wipe our faces. So old Captain Halsey came up and said
'Splendid' and asked if we could do some entertainment. Well,
we had seen stage shows, comedians, and the like, and we did
an hour's stage show. And that about sealed it.

Emperors of Jazz, Hammersmith, 1936. *Left to right*: Abe 'Pops' Clare (string bs); Yorke de Souza (p); Reg Amore, Freddie Greenslade (tb); Arthur Dibbin, Leslie 'Jiver' Hutchinson, Leslie Thompson (t); Ken Johnson; Winnie Cooper (vcls); Louis Stephenson (alto sax); Bertie King (tenor sax); Robert Mumford-Taylor (alto sax); Tom Wilson (dms); Joe Deniz (g). The two trombonists have been 'blacked up' – they were white.

We had no band name: it changed, but generally it had 'Jamaican' in the title. Ken Johnson was a stick wagger – he was no musician.[17] Somehow his name got put out there on the posters, but I think by this time we were called the Emperors of Jazz. Our opening number usually was 'White Heat', an American tune that had a fine arrangement which allowed the sections to play: one moment the saxes would stand up, the next the trumpets – very spectacular. After about six months Ken Johnson came up, round about the time we were to go on – the other band was about to finish and changeover time was due – and said he had signed a new contract. It was really tense after our performance, because we all asked Ken to repeat his comment. 'Have you signed a contract?' the lads asked me, and I told them I hadn't. The dispute broke up the band. At this time we had Wally Bowen who was from the police band in

Ken Johnson and the Jamaican Emperors of Jazz (courtesy Graham Langley).

Trinidad, I think on trumpet, and Bruce Vanderpoye, a coloured South African, on bass.

Ken went off to the West Indies and recruited some new fellows from Trinidad, and they came over in mid-1937 and that became the Ken Johnson West Indian Swing Band. Only 'Jiver' Hutchinson and Yorke de Souza went with Ken when the Old Florida Club band split. Until I saw the picture I had no idea that Yorke went off to Australia in 1937. Of course I heard about the band – Dave Wilkins, Dave Williams, George Roberts, and Carl Barriteau – West Indians, but none of them from Jamaica.

I have told you that Duke was tough, but I haven't told you about Benny Carter. I don't regard Duke as the grand-daddy as I think that Carter has to be the number one. He was the most outstanding coloured musician. He had a wide experience, was polished, could play so many instruments so well, and was above all a fantastic arranger. He worked in Hollywood. Carter always had good men but he never had the luck. I have always let circumstances guide me, so, when my band broke up after Ken Johnson signed that contract, I didn't start another one. When I was double-crossed I dropped it.

Carter kept on trying; he just never got the publicity that Duke and the others got.

In the 1930s I used to see Marcus Garvey at Speakers' Corner. At that time you would see coloured chaps, Indian students on their soap boxes, attacking Britain's colonial system, and Marcus would stand there, watching them, with an expression on his face that indicated to me that he had done that, what – ten and more years ago – in America. When I mentioned the Ward Theatre in Kingston, back in 1927, I didn't tell you that I'm sure that the owners would have been pleased to let their theatre to Marcus, for it often stood empty when visiting shows were not available. Some local fellows with enterprise might put on some thing, so it was available for hire. As for the UNIA band, I had no knowledge of it and must presume that it was a pick-up group. But I have no recollection of Marcus in Jamaica. I must have been working and so was unable to attend. I had no race consciousness at all; even the influence of Garvey's newspaper only dented my attitudes. I was a product of my background. Jamaica was dominated by a culture from England and America, and like many I accepted it without thinking. Marcus Garvey was responsible for my awakening, and for so many people like me. And that's why he is Jamaica's national hero, and why so many West Indians are interested in the man and his ideas.

Seeing that picture of Sam Manning reminds me: yes, I did know that he was involved with Marcus Garvey's wife, one of the wives, in some way. Sam Manning was in *The Sun Never Sets* at Drury Lane. Those shows that had large coloured casts never really did well. The promoter would get Paul Robeson or someone of quality to head the show, and the rest would be hired because of their colour. Almost anything that had a large number of coloured artists was never a success, because the other actors were so poor. Remember I was working in the top shows, so I know what I am talking about. Will Garland's *Brown Birds* was good, and so were the *Blackbirds* shows. But so many of those shows were bad. And the individual artists suffered, as theatrical agents hardly distinguished between coloured artists; only the giants, like Robeson, Elisabeth Welch, and Josephine Baker, avoided the stigma resulting from poor quality all-coloured shows.

My band broke up in 1937, around the time I made those records with Benny Carter. I was the only other coloured fellow at those sessions, at the Maida Vale studios. There was Freddy Gardner, Harry Hayes, Tommy McQuater, and George Chisholm. As with Spike I played both the trumpet and the trombone. Carter was really excellent; but I must hand it to Bertie King, and not just because he had gone to Alpha, that he might well be compared to Carter. Certainly as a jazz player Bertie's ideas matched those of Coleman Hawkins, the great tenor man.

After the band broke up I went back to Cochran and worked with Jessie Matthews and Sonnie Hale in their shows, and on tour.[18] We went to Brighton and Preston, and then I did another Cochran show in town. In 1938 Fats Waller came over, and of course I saw him. He was often in the clubs, and he would play when asked, and then off to a party, and so we would end up drinking whisky in his flat in Jermyn Street, right into the wee small hours. Fats was a dreamer – his life was sort of floating on air. His act, his stage act, was so much a part of him, so individualistic, that it was pure Fats. Fine players always have that ethereal quality, for they have such powerful imaginations. He was often playing at being a funny man: reaching for the Scotch – 'have another drink'. But the real Fats was a dreamer. So the people he worked with had to be disciplinarians to get him to perform on time. Yet, after his Palladium show, after work, he would go off to the clubs, and there he would play for nothing. At the Nest Club, in the small hours of the morning, around four or five o'clock, he played one set of forty-five minutes – free. In that way he was the opposite of Louis.

Fats was friendly with Spencer Williams, the New Orleans composer. I had seen Spencer in the music publishers in London in the 1930s, for he had been in England a long time – certainly a good few years when I met him. I saw him in the Charing Cross Road, and would stop to say hello. He was distant – aloof. I can't recall seeing him in the Nest, where most of the coloured artists would be seen; he was something of a recluse. I always had the impression that he was a sporadic worker, producing one or two songs here and then nothing for months. He had a gift but it didn't flow all the time. In the theatrical shows there would be chaps working away, presenting fresh books for consideration, new tunes, songs, routines, and so on; Spencer Williams wasn't like that at all.

Macfarlane, the variety agent, got a boys' band together. That was typical of that time, for there were bands of women, of boys, and all-coloured bands. Novelty attractions. Well, Woolf Phillips, whose brother was Sid, who led his own band after the war, was a trombonist in this lads' band, and so was Lad Busby – that was his real name, although he played in a lads' band. I coached them from 1936 into 1937, and I am proud to say that most of them became professional musicians. It was a novelty stage band, and was quite popular, but of course the boys grew up!

There were other coloured musicians around in the thirties. There was Errol Barrow, a pianist (from Trinidad, I think) who came on the scene in 1936 or 1937. Then Alpha Cottage School had produced Clinton Maxwell, a drummer. He was a little younger than me, but we had been there at the same time. He was tall and skinny. I think he came on his own to England, after he left Alpha in the early 1920s. Freddy Grant was from a police band in Trinidad or British Guiana. Guitarist Lauderic Caton was from Trinidad, and Brylo Ford was from the West

Indies.[19] Those two, with Grant and Maxwell, recorded with
Cyril Blake at Jig's Club in late 1941. Edmundo Ros, who was
often working at Jig's Club – which is where he must have met
Waller, and so got on the recording session with Dave Wilkins
and Chisholm – didn't have a band of his own in 1938. Wilkins
came from Trinidad but he was born in Barbados, and he came
over to join Ken Johnson. Ros used to play the drums at the
Nest, so that must have been where Fats heard him. And I saw
the Mills Brothers at Jig's Club.

I've told you about the little Harlem of the Armstrong bus,
and the way in which Afro-Americans regarded me as a black
Englishman, but there was a lot of contact between West
Indians in London. They would define themselves by stating
where they were from – Montserrat, Antigua, Barbados, and so
on. That was for my benefit, so that I could ask 'Have you ever
been to Jamaica?' and so avoid referring to Kingston with the
other fellow having no idea what I was talking about. And the
British-born coloured artists, like Dennis Walton, who played
with me in the Edmundo Ros group, and the Deniz brothers
and Mumford-Taylor had no idea of life in the West Indies, of
course. But the thing that dominated was the pigment, especially in dance music.

In the 1930s all the dance groups aimed at being American.
The modern popular music today is guitars and amplifiers,
but back in the 1930s it was saxophones and trumpets, and
you played for dancers. The dance band records of the
Americans were greatly admired, and those jazz bands were
really regarded as the best. The instrumental technique and the
arrangements of the Americans were so good that every dance
musician in Europe aimed at being American. Black or white,
you aimed at being American. So the 'all-coloured' bands aimed
to be American, and we coloured chaps, united by our colour
and by our ambitions, had a group feeling even if we came from
Guiana, Jamaica, Africa, Barbados, Cardiff or London.

Old Florida Club 1937: Wally Bowen (t); Yorke de Souza (p); Leslie Thompson, Arthur Dibbin (t); Tom Wilson (d); Robert Mumford-Taylor (saxes); Joe Deniz (g); Louis Stephenson (reeds); Bruce Vanderpoye (string bs); Bertie King (saxes).

Shortly after Leslie Hutchinson – 'Jiver' Hutchinson, the trumpeter – came to London with Bertie King, he told me that he had a fiancée in Jamaica. He asked me should he sort of cut the strings or send for her. I told him that if you really wanted respect from the whites you must have your own woman from the West Indies. There would be no criticism. If you got yourself a white girl some would respect you, and some would think that she had let the side down. So she came over. Poor old Leslie hired some heap of a truck, years later this was, and when it crashed the insurance blamed him. He was killed in the accident, of course, poor fellow.[20] And I believe that he lost – no, his widow, of course – lost the house and everything. I saw his son when I was in the probation service, years later. After Leslie's wife came to England I invited them to a church service in Highgate, and they came, but that was the only time I saw his wife. That would have been just about the time that war broke out.

I had become a more placid sort of fellow after the Ken Johnson debacle, for it made me think. Where do I go from here? I remembered my childhood at Alpha and that atmosphere – how happy I had been, believing and trusting in God, which I did as a child does, without thinking. But the outcome of that trust and belief was that I had got my profession. So I took stock of the situation, and decided to be a bit more serious, and certainly to hold no grudge against Ken or the manager and agent. But my first reactions were furious, of course. I became so angry and embittered that I sought a way out. Being spiteful or full of revenge wouldn't get you composure. And I am grateful that this double-cross gave me a chance to take stock of my position and to make the choice that I did, for it had far-reaching consequences.

By the end of the 1930s the music scene in Britain had changed because of the nature of the jazz that was played. It was transformed from English jazz to American jazz. The American recordings that had come to England had their full effect, and everyone was aiming to be American, and to a great degree they succeeded. The polish of the sectional performances of the orchestras increased and the phrasing became quite Americanised. This was due to records and the visits of individuals – Ellington, Calloway, Waller, Garland Wilson – most of their British fans were musicians. After their performances to the paying public at a theatre these chaps would go on to parties which had a musical clientele. Naturally the Americans gravitated to the Nest, Jig's, the Bag O' Nails, and such night spots. At those places they met their fans – white musicians. So, in that decade the bands in England became very polished, American-style. They captured the heart of rhythmic music – to swing – so the listener would tap his foot to the music.

4

Bombardier, Cellist

When war was declared in September 1939 all the theatres closed. There was the blackout, fear of bombing, and the call up [draft] which reduced the ranks of staff, stage hands, orchestras, and turns. I got back to London from the Cochran circuit and joined Edmundo Ros. He was from Trinidad but said he was from Venezuela. He formed a little group, with me on the string bass, Dennis Walton played the trumpet, Robert English, who became Roberto Inglez, Frank Deniz, and Dudley Misso. We did Latin American music! Playing the bass, as I told my son years later, is more than a musical job, because you are standing up when all or most of the other musicians are sitting down. You must sway with the beat, and be a showman. We worked at the Mayfair Hotel, as a cabaret show, for there was a need for entertainment, with the threat of war, invasion, death, and so on. We did live broadcasts, and Ros introduced the dance steps – samba, mambo, and so on – to the audience and taught them to dance to the music we supplied. Some people are not backward at trying anything and it soon caught on. I was really surprised.

I was with Edmundo Ros until I was called up in 1942. I can truly say that we started Latin American dance music in London! One of the BBC studio managers was Cecil Madden,

Edmundo Ros' band 1940: Leslie Thompson, Dudley Misso, Edmundo Ros, Dennis Walton, Roberto Inglez.

and he had lived in South America, and he liked our music. The Criterion Theatre at Piccadilly Circus was being used as a studio for broadcasting, and we performed there. We were broadcasting at least once a week in 1940 and 1941.

Our base was the Coconut Grove in Piccadilly, and so we could grab taxis, go to the Criterion, tiptoe in as others were on the air, and then we would be on. And those broadcasts opened a lot of doors for us. I had done a couple of television broadcasts before the war closed down that service – after the Ken Johnson debacle at the Old Florida Club. It is a pity that Decca never got to record that band, because then there would be evidence to support my belief that the later Ken Johnson band, the one that got bombed at the Café de Paris in March 1941 – when Ken Johnson was killed – sounded the same as mine. I am sure that no West Indian band in London had that sound, which died with Ken in the blitz. It had taken months to produce.

At the Old Florida Club I was getting twenty pounds a week or more, and the band got fifteen pounds a week or eighteen. I advertised George Scarth's new trumpet for him, as a favour.[1] When I was with Armstrong I was getting twelve to fifteen, but I don't remember if that was after I had sent money home. It is important to be paid well in show business because there could be times when there are no jobs. I always felt sorry for the coloured dancers who could get work when there was an all-coloured show on, but they spent months going round the agents, drawing blanks. Will Garland's English wife was the brains behind his business; and Spencer Williams wrote such good songs that he was always welcome. Reginald Foresythe, the coloured composer, titled one composition 'Serenade for a Wealthy Widow' because he was looking for exactly that kind of assistance – he was broke.

Well, I kept working with Edmundo Ros right until I was called up in 1942. I was now forty, so the military weren't that anxious to have me, but they needed people in the anti-aircraft defences, and so I got my call-up papers for the Royal Artillery and off to Devizes I went. This time I was serving King George V's son, and another change was that my new army number was twice as long as my former one – I can't for the life of me recall what it was, but it was eight numbers. And so I was back in the army again.

Before I get into my wartime years I'll tell you that I moved from Marchmont Street to Sussex Gardens around 1936. I mean I tried to move. I went to the estate agents in Maida Vale, and a fellow took me to this flat, to have a look around and make up my mind, and it was fine, and agreed, and so we went back to the office to sign the papers. His boss saw us, and called the fellow in, and when he came out he was very embarrassed and shuffled from one foot to the other, and finally said 'I'm sorry, Mr Thompson.' The Church Commissioners owned those properties, and they had a clause that no coloured person could be a tenant. So I didn't move. And to think that several of those nightclub hostesses lived there, and I worked in the clubs and knew how they got the rent money that the estate agent and the Church Commissioners were only too pleased to receive.

I got divorced around 1938 or 1939, I think; I was living in Bayswater, deeper into Paddington, then. When Leslie Brown mentioned that Barbados fellow his father called 'the Emperor Jones' he may well have been describing a fellow I knew, who lived a few yards from me – a hundred yards – along the same street. I can't recall, but was it Chepstow Road? He fitted that well-dressed, boarding-house keeper that Leslie Brown remembered. I met this man just about the time that war broke out. He was down on his luck then. We spoke a couple of times. He sold me a lovely suitcase because he was broke, and knew that I was working, and had the money. Some time after that I got a message that he wanted to see me, that he had something for me. Certainly he wanted to see me most urgently. He had a letter for me: I can't think how he got it, unless the postman delivered it to him because he was coloured and the envelope had Jamaican stamps on it. But how it got to Paddington I don't know. Anyway, it was my life insurance. I had taken out a twenty-year policy with the Jamaican Mutual Life Assurance Company, an endowment policy, and it had matured. I had forgotten all about it. In fact I had paid it during my Kingston days, and a few times in England, but I thought that it had lapsed. And in that strange way I got my money. I can't recall the fellow's name at all, but I remember he was my colour, had a boarding house after the war, and maybe during the war. I believe that he got elected on the Paddington council at the end of the war, around 1946.

When I was living in Paddington or Bayswater, whatever

you want to call it, I often walked along the park and passed Speakers' Corner, where the Edgware Road meets Hyde Park. There I saw Prince Monolulu: I think he was from the West Indies, but he had been in London for years. He liked to be the centre of attraction, and as well as his racecourse work with the famous 'I got an 'orse' tips, he was well established in the West End. Complete with feathers and that lucky horseshoe, he tried to impress recently arrived West Indian lads by a sophisticated air of knowing his way round. His language was terrible. So I saw Monolulu – Prince Ras Monolulu to give him his full bogus title – on odd days. I also saw Tunde Alakija, who had married an English girl and lived with their two children near Holloway. I saw a lot of Fela Sowande, who also came from Nigeria. He studied at the Royal College of Organists; he played the Hammond organ at clubs where Adelaide Hall sang. Jazz on the electric organ was really a novelty in the thirties. She and Fela made records, too, of course. I think that all the time Adelaide Hall was in London Fela played with her. And then there was his *African Suite*, which was broadcast by us, the band that became Ken Johnson's. That was a semi-classical composition with African rhythms, which was quite a novelty at that time. It would still be a novelty today, in fact. Years later Fela conducted it in the States.

Well, I was playing with Edmundo Ros when my call-up papers came. How anyone knew that I was in England still defeats me, but just as that insurance cheque shows, the authorities have ways. I had been a member of the Musicians' Union, I paid income tax, I ran a car – I was there on paper, and so the papers found me. At that time, if there was any reason for not serving, you could go before a tribunal. I was working with Ros at the Coconut Grove, and Diana the manageress said that my string bass was an integral part of the band. So I went before the tribunal, in Chapel Street off the Edgware Road, and the magistrates listened, and deliberated, and decided that my services in the army would be more beneficial to the war effort than playing at the Coconut Grove, so that was that.

Mind you it wasn't an easy job, being a musician in wartime London. I can remember Ken Johnson coming in to where we were playing, and having a nice bottle of Spanish wine with his dinner, before going off just about ten to work at the Café de Paris. We were playing at Martini's Restaurant, which we did before moving along to the Coconut Grove for the late-night stint, and the stairs were almost above our heads, so we could see the people come and go. So we saw Ken, in his lovely white suit, go off to lead the lads – George Roberts, Dave Wilkins, 'Jiver' Hutchinson, Joey Deniz, and the others. I had peace in my mind, through my Christian faith, since the debacle, so it was no problem to shake Ken's hand. And soon after we got to the Coconut Grove we were told that a German bomb had landed on the Café de Paris and the whole lot was gone. Ken's girlfriend came in and said, 'It's finished – the band's wiped out.'

They had advertised the place as bomb-proof, but they didn't realise that the dance floor was under the cinema, and so that bomb went straight through the roof of the cinema and into the dance hall and Ken was killed, so was Dave Williams, and the others were injured. The death roll was over thirty, I believe. That was March 1941. And only a few weeks later singer Al Bowlly, the Greek singer, was dead in a raid. I didn't feel any animosity towards Ken; the change in my life that thinking about those events in 1937 had brought about was such that I wished him well, but the bomb did him in. I went to the funeral at Golders Green. I felt sorry for him; for he was such a nice boy, but he wanted money, and he got led off without being aware of the consequences. The utter futility of fame and popularity: it completely changed my whole outlook on life. I had come to England to get success, to be well-known, and to get lots of money. The unknown, as it were, came through, and hit me like that. People had been crazy over our coloured band – so successful. What price – what value, is success?

Those musicians who didn't get into uniform had the war to face – ration books, blackout, the loss of loved ones, and the raids – so many raids that the anti-aircraft regiments needed anyone they could get, and they got me.

I got my papers and took the train to Devizes. At the station there was a three-ton truck, and this bombardier called out 'Anyone for Wiltshire barracks?' and twenty or so of us stepped over. We got in the back and looked at each other, all wondering what would happen next. At the barracks we all got out and were directed to a hut and told to pick out a bed. A chap came in and gave us a paper, telling us to fill in details of our education, civvy street job, and experience. After a while he collected them, and after another ten or twenty minutes he came in and called out 'Leslie Thompson.' So off I went, asking no questions. The adjutant wanted to see me: I was going wrong already! Captain Ball stood up when I came in and shook my hand. 'So glad to see you, we've got a band here and we want a man to handle it. Would you take charge?' They were semi-pros, you know, the weekend dance band chaps, who could play sax, drums, and so on. Actually I [had] thought about my trumpet, and realised that if I didn't take it then any playing opportunity would be lost or I would be playing some ancient wreck of a horn; and so I had brought it. The adjutant's clerk played the piano. There were, let me see – saxophone, drums, no – two saxophones, drums, trumpet, trombone, piano, and bass. The saxes were supposed to double on the clarinet, and I was playing my trumpet. So it was an eight-piece band. There was a concert that week in the NAAFI, so that afternoon I had

Leslie Thompson
back in uniform,
1942

to rehearse. That afternoon I got my new kit – my number wasn't even dry when I started with this new band.

Some of the boys didn't have much of an idea, but we worked at it. The performers were all in the NAAFI, and the camp heard that they had Edmundo Ros' trumpet player. Funny that, for I had been playing mostly bass with him, but that gives you an idea of how Ros had taken the nation by storm. And they all came to the NAAFI to look. We started, and stopped, and did this, and changed that, and after half an hour we were getting a bit of a swing to it, and so we took a break. One fellow, who was a clerk – a fellow in his forties, who didn't look like a soldier for his uniform was so unnatural – well, he came over and said 'My name is Hudson. I've never noticed such a remarkable change in a group of musicians as you have produced this afternoon.' By the end of the week, for the Friday night concert, we could do three or four or five numbers. I played a solo – classical style, trumpet voluntary. This was by way of a change from the jazz sound. Hudson was an organist, a fine organist, and he played the piano. I drew him in to play the non-jazz things. Our concert went down well, and the band was the high spot.

The next weekend we had to go to another camp, in the same area of Wiltshire. We gave a performance and the officer came up and spoke to his men, saying 'It is not good for us to covet, but this band does give such satisfaction that I would like to have it here.' On Mondays we would go to a searchlight unit. You see, there were airforce people, and all sorts, in that area. And we played at a dance, once a week. The searchlight and radar people included ATS girls, so dances were possible. I suppose the infantry had no dances – all those fellows. And in Devizes there were the heavy anti-aircraft regiments, and the radar, and also the Wiltshire Regiment, which had a proper regimental band. Their bandmaster was a double medallist from Kneller Hall. He had got a medal as a bandsman, and another when he was training as a band director. He must have been at Kneller Hall before I went there. Sometimes he would drag me in as a soloist in his regimental band, but I was actually in the Royal Artillery, Gunner Thompson, R.A.

We had done our basic training, learning about guns, too. This took three or four weeks, something like that. The intake was posted to a particular battery, to serve as gunners. In the artillery the novice soldier is a gunner and the trained soldier is a lance bombardier which is the same as a lance corporal; then if you got two stripes you would be a corporal in the infantry but in the Royal Artillery you were a bombardier. But I was required in the garrison, because of the band. So I became a member of the permanent staff, as a driver. I drove anything from a small car to a huge truck. I was a member of the artillery's motor transport division. There were thousands of troops in the area, and air force too. A few thousand fellows and girls, and there were the Wellington bombers which would fly off on bombing raids over Europe. There were plenty of instructors, old and experienced sergeants, and so the ignorant had little opportunity to show their stupidity. So there was no trouble over race. In fact all the time I was in the artillery I only saw one other coloured soldier. And then I didn't speak to him. We had dances at the battery – in Portsmouth, by this time – and I was on the stage. This coloured sergeant was dancing away. A lovely dancer. Of course there were the coloured Americans, but I didn't really meet any. In Portsmouth I was the only coloured fellow in the whole brigade.

Well, when the Americans came over the barracks were allocated to them and we had to disperse, and there were postings all over the place. I went off to Wales. But I hadn't had it easy in the motor transport section, for we had to clean the trucks, and those cold winters, driving across the iron-like ploughed fields, and putting your hands in icy diesel fuel. Boy! And our sergeant was such a stickler for details that often we were the last in the queue at the NAAFI for tea and cigarettes. But I had a cozy job at first, going to the coke dump in a three-tonner, with a fatigue party. They loaded the truck, and I drove it to each of the huts, for coke was the fuel. And the cookhouse people would give me a big mug of tea, with that Carnation milk, and I could hardly refuse, so I got quite portly. The amount of tea I used to drink – lots of tea.

So I was in Devizes for a year, until the Americans came. Our group, which was 160 Anti-Aircraft Regiment, had two batteries, 556 and 557, and it was to 556 I was posted. I had to learn how to fire. The training was at Ty Croes in Anglesey, in Wales, for six weeks. After this shooting practice I went on leave. The training was very interesting, for I was setting the fuses. Others had different tasks. One man sets the height, and another sets the bearing, of the target. These are the layers. The man who fires is the number one, and usually is the sergeant. There were ammunition carriers, and the fuse setter

– that was me. My speed became the talk of the camp, so much so that after a couple of weeks the corps commander came over a few times to watch us shoot. We shot at the sleeve, the target dragged behind – a long way behind – a plane. There would be shouts – bearing, height, and fuse – set – loaded – and fire. I had to shout 'set' when I had set the fuse. And it was just a fraction after the fuse setting had been told to me. They could test the accuracy of the setting because the shell would explode near the sleeve. I was well praised. I think there were ten thousand troops in that training area. There were different regiments. After the basics you went in for instruction on dials, and then on the radar, and I must say that my beginning as a fuse setter was an asset. And, as well as that speed, there was always the trumpet. Each regiment had a chaplain, and the Sunday morning divine service was special. Now a piano in a large NAAFI hall was too quiet, so my trumpet was requested, and I added to my reputation in that way. I also played in the hymn singing of a Sunday evening. It kept my lip in, and me out of mischief.

It was when I was at Devizes that I met Frank Williams again. He was a bombardier, and played his trombone in a band somewhere in Hampshire. And that band came to Devizes to give a concert, and so I met him again. I saw him after he was demobbed; somehow I found out that he was ill, and so I went to see him in hospital. He had high blood pressure and he died not long after. A lovely tone on his trombone; a lovely home-loving lad, and so very, very English.

With Ros we were well paid, and the military paid next to nothing, so I drew on my savings. I didn't spend very much, for I hardly took a drink and I had given up smoking. When we played at the army dances they put chalk and shavings of candles on the floor, to make it easy to slide and glide, but after the dance started it was like a fog: and the taste would be in your throat. So we got free drinks – I always had a glass of shandy. A pint of lemonade and beer, which took some of the taste away. As for smoking, I can tell you that I started again in the army. It was the Christmas Day dinner, when the tradition has the officers serve the men. This ATS officer gave me a cigarette, and she was responsible for me starting again. After a few days I thought what a fool I was. Mind you, it was just puff, puff – I never inhaled it. I was in the YMCA quiet room, reading, and I found myself putting down an excellent book just to light a cigarette. I thought: what was I doing with this cigarette? I had a large cigarette case, with two sides, but I never did smoke a lot and even being late for the NAAFI handouts, because of Sgt Skipp's high standards back in the motor transport section, never left me with an empty case. So I called out to the boys and they rushed over and cleaned out my case. I had a cigarette some time later. That would be in Croydon, when my regiment was brought up to man the defences – from Staines to Sheerness – against the rocket bombs. I was a sergeant, and it was at Raynes Park in south west London. I was in the sergeants' mess when the colonel came in, and offered his cigarettes around. He passed the case to me first, and I took one – without thinking. And then he came round with his lighter, and looked at me, oddly, because he knew I didn't smoke. I tasted that wretched cigarette for two weeks. It was the last cigarette I had.

When the war broke out, Tony, my son, went to Ireland. We had employed a nanny, a lovely lady named Kitty Marum, as his nurse, and she looked after him when my marriage broke up. She had to go off to Ireland, and asked me if she could take my lad with her. So off to Wicklow he went. Ireland was neutral in the war, of course. He was there until he was six or so, maybe eight; certainly he started school in Ireland. There were plenty of children and Kitty's relatives. When he came back he stayed with a minister friend in Worthing, and from there he was looked after in Sheringham in Norfolk. He was ten or twelve then. And when he was fourteen he came back to London, towards the end of the 1940s. I was living in Maida Vale then, and he stayed with me until I decided to get him into the band of the Royal Artillery.

I was in Portsmouth in 1943 and 1944. It was before the V-bombs, before the doodle bugs. I was posted to London for those rocket bombs.[2] By now I was Lance Bombardier Thompson. I had been in Southampton, and was into my second year in the artillery, when I got my promotion. And then I went to Storrington, in Sussex, where there were thousands of Canadians, for a course, for potential sergeants. There were two hundred lance bombardiers there, and I was one of a handful that got a distinction. I was distinguished for something else, too. The day – I'll never forget it – was when the big shots came down and the results were announced. When they called my name I shot up – I was in the front, and the only coloured chap there, of course – and grabbed my forage cap. They were pointed, and worn at an angle. Well, as I stood up I put my cap on, and I could hear some whispers; and when I went up to the officer he was smiling, and when I sat down I realised I had put it on back-to-front, with the badge at the rear. Only when I took it off did I realise. Distinguished – indeed.

There was an infinitesimal amount of the colour business. We had an officer who was South African, and he was posted to the headquarters of the battery. He was paying out: he had the money, and someone would call your name, and up to the front you went. Salute, take the pay, and go back. He was looking down when I saluted, and when he looked up he said that I hadn't saluted him. The sergeant told him I had. He was the only one. Then, at Croydon they came to take some pictures and the brigadier pointed at me and said, 'We don't want *that* in the picture,' but my officer made a point, at the dance that evening, of bringing this silly man to the front of the bandstand and standing right in front of me so he could hear and see how *that* could play the trumpet.

Now my moment of military grandeur. I had been to the artillery training camp at Manobier in South Wales, on a course. There I had realised that gunnery was an art. The officer instructors had this gift, and I was very much a time-waster, because no matter how I swotted it wasn't in me. Those fellows were really very skilled. The brigadier who had been at Manobier was transferred to be commander of the area where my battery was. He had devised this drill for shooting high-flying planes, which he had taken to the War Office, who had rejected it. He wasn't put off by this official rejection, but put his drill into standing orders. So everyone in his command followed his special drill, despite the official opinion of it. Now we had a lieutenant, a Jewish fellow, well-anglicised, by the name of Dowling. He was a tall chap, very good as a gunner, and he drilled us. A battery would have up to eight guns, but ours had five or six, I think; as sergeant I was responsible for one gun, but Dowling was responsible for the battery. He made us work – and he would yell at us if we made a mistake – and we really practised the new drill. It was in the middle of the afternoon that one of the two spotters saw this German plane.

The spotters were girls – women, I should say – who served in the ATS. Miss Bolland and another were in the usual position, facing each other, so that they could see 180 degrees in front of them, covering a full circle with two spotters. And they looked up from horizon to directly above, ninety degrees. It was like an apple, cut in half and placed skin side up on a plate. Cut it in half again, and each apple segment was the area covered by each spotter. She spotted a little puff, just like a small cloud, but thought it might be smoke from an aircraft.

Sgt Thompson on the anti-aircraft battery, Portsmouth, 1943

Her colleague agreed that it could be a plane, and they rang the alarum bell. Within a few minutes we were at the battery, covers off, and ready. The radar picked up the plane from the bearing given by the spotters, and confirmed that it wasn't one of our planes. So we fired. There wasn't time to fire more than three or four shells from each gun before we got it. That Messerschmidt 109 G was seven miles up. I should refer to a technical manual of gunnery, but I think that the shells took from ten to fourteen seconds to get up there: 34 thousand feet.

So we shot down the highest flying German plane over Britain. And everyone was interested. General Sir Frederick

Pile came along: he was in charge of British anti-aircraft defences, and he came along with his brass hats. He was a very nice little man. As sergeant, in charge of the team on the gun, I had to meet all these people, with the other sergeants and their gunners. Of course none of us knew who had fired the shell, because we were all firing. Those fine girls had to be good, as we fired on the calculations based on their data. So that was my moment of glory in the war.

The battery was isolated, so we all got to know each other and mixed well together. There were two hundred people and so this isolation was different to the crowded life in infantry regiments. Some people you disliked intensely, and some you liked a great deal. We would chat, or read, or just think: waiting for the alarum bell. We made our own amusements, cards and snooker. There weren't many exciting moments apart from the firing. This was in Portsmouth, and we were the first battery back on the site after the previous lot had been bombed. Although the site had been repaired there were plenty of signs to show where the others had been when the bombs landed: that was food for thought.

I think I was in Shirley, near Croydon, on D-Day, when the Allies landed in France. I was in the Royal Artillery then, June 1944, but soon after that I joined Stars in Battledress. When the Americans came over, and scattered all over the place, they had the benefit of British bands and entertainers, but the Second Front brought all manner of US brass hats to Britain, and with them came Glenn Miller's band of the American Expeditionary Force. This set the British off. Of course we already had ENSA, Stars in Battledress, and other groups to entertain the troops and the factory workers. Miller was an officer – Major Glenn Miller. The band of the British expeditionary force was led by Sgt Maj. George Melachrino. I heard about these developments on the grapevine, for I took my leaves in London, and there someone told me that Stars in Battledress were looking for people. I went to this office near the river in Chelsea, where they all knew me from civvy street. So I got transferred. I was still Sgt Thompson, R.A., but now I lived out of barracks, as a sort of private soldier. We rehearsed a lot. The big band was the pool, and little dribbles formed into bands; there were any number of bands by the end of 1944. My outfit was Latin American, and we dressed to suit this. We were called Buenos Aires 6-5000 after the American hit song.[3] We numbered a dozen: three saxophones, a piano, drum, string bass, guitar, a girl singer, and I played the trumpet. And there were three lads, actors and comedians: one was Czech. One of the sax players was Cyril Harling, from Tagg's Island. We were all professional musicians and some were symphonic players. Did you know that the RAF had a symphony orchestra during the war?

I went to Germany and then to Norway, at the end of the war, after May 1945. In fact Winston Churchill's plane took off from the aerodrome just before our plane left for Germany. I can remember the lights coming on after the Germans surrendered. I was on a train, going up to London, from south London I think, and suddenly we saw lights in the houses. The blackout curtains weren't needed anymore, after six years. Someone wrote a song about it.

In Germany the troops were absolutely isolated from the natives. There was a certain amount of tension and insecurity about the future, so the Germans were left alone and the troops were kept away. Physically Germany was a revelation, for as we flew over the cities which had been blitzed by the RAF you could see houses without roofs or windows, and rubble everywhere. It made you think that the Germans had started this war and had got the answer all right. Mind you, we didn't feel glad – or sorry, either. We went on to Norway, where I found the people to be very friendly and unsophisticated. We were in Oslo, Bergen, Tromso, and Stavanger. Norway had been occupied by the Germans but their government had moved to London and by the time we were there everyone was pretty pro-British. All the time, in Germany and Norway, we ate army rations, with a small but sure ration of whisky, cigarettes and chocolate. We travelled together in our group, and when we had a base it was in an army camp, from which we would travel to entertain military personnel in Norway and Germany. There were opportunities for walking out and so you could drift around and in that way I bought a German camera outside the Reichstag in Berlin. Really we didn't meet many people other than the audiences. It was isolated, in the same way that the anti-aircraft work had been.

I was demobbed in 1946, at Chelsea barracks near Sloane Square. I took a bus up to Archer Street and within twenty minutes I got a job working at a nightclub in Berkeley Square. It was owned by a millionaire named John, a Swede, I think; he had made his fortune in matches. I worked with Billy Duffy, who was now called Ramon Lopez. It was that Latin American music, that Edmundo Ros had made so popular before the war got going. Now I was playing my trumpet and not the bass. From Mayfair I moved to the Embassy, and then to Ciro's which is where I played for the present Queen.

I was living in Maida Vale, at Clifton Gardens. It was there that my son joined me. Robert Mumford-Taylor and I worked together at the Cossack in Jermyn Street in the early 1950s, and that was my last job in music. Three lawyers from Hungary, who had been in London for years, owned that place. I believe that they had bought several prime properties in that area of Piccadilly, including Prince's Restaurant. There was Saki and Jaro; the third name I can't recall. Well, Dr Saki liked me and anytime there was a change in the band he insisted that I was kept on as trumpeter, and so I settled in there into the 1950s.

After the war I no longer worked in the theatres, touring, or making records, and as my dance band work was from eight in the evening I decided to improve my musical knowledge. I enrolled at the Guildhall School of Music, where I studied during the day. There were periods when you had to wait for a lesson or a lecture, and we would jaw in the canteen over a cup of tea, or rehearse. I was playing the cello in the orchestra, and conducting, too. Actually my course was conducting. The orchestra was made up of teachers, pupils, and professionals. We did Beethoven, Haydn, Mozart, Tchaikovsky, and other masters. I was at the Guildhall [School] nearly every weekday for two years. Although the tuition was seldom more than two or three hours a day, I killed time in various ways, especially as there were always plenty of violin players looking for a cellist for quartet and quintet work – just as it had been with Vera Manley and her friends in the 1920s. I got the silver medal because, as the examiner wrote, I was too quick. I sailed through the examination paper and left out too many details. The girl who won the gold was just a single point ahead of me. She was a West Indian, a coloured girl – a pianist. This was 1947 or 1948. You can look it up in the Guildhall records.

One occasion, when I was killing time in the dining room, this girl cellist heard me remark 'The princess was in last night,' and she asked me what I did at night. 'Nocturnal research' I replied! I was keeping her in the dark on my dance band work – Latin American music at Ciro's and classical during the day. We played 'Brazil' and 'Begin the Beguine' – that Latin American stuff. You know, playing at those society places was hard work, for we started at eight and packed up when the last dancer had had enough, often ten hours later. Hardly the activities approved of by earnest students at the Guildhall.

There were one or two reunions of the ack-ack battery, but the years after the war had their own problems; all sorts of things were in short supply, and there was rationing of food and so on. And we were scattered to the winds; we never met up again. And so it was with those West Indian chaps from before the war. I had no idea that Dave Wilkins played with Ted Heath's orchestra, yet I knew that Heath's band was a high-class and popular group. And as for Joe Appleton recording in Germany, well! I saw Dunbar in Store Street, coming out of the post office when I was going in, in the 1940s, but I didn't see him again until the Coleridge-Taylor concert in May 1985.[4] I didn't get the musical papers, like the *Melody Maker*, and I was busy on lots of other matters. I had my cello, and the conducting course at the Guildhall [School] for two years, and then I had my son to look after. I got him into the band of the Royal Artillery – and I had to get back into the religious community, as it were – and this led to all sorts of contacts and eventually to a new job.

Of course I knew about Learie Constantine and his law suit against that hotel in Southampton Row. He had booked in by phone, and got a cable to confirm this, but the receptionist said they didn't take coloured guests. So he asked to see the manager, and he told Learie that the hotel's policy was to refuse coloured guests, despite the cable. So Learie sued them – and won. He had been a professional cricketer up in Lancashire before the war, and had some job working amongst the West Indian labourers who were recruited for the war industries up there. He was from Trinidad. Years later he studied law, and eventually became Lord Constantine and sat in the House of Lords.

I knew about the ship, the *Empire Windrush*. There was a little bit in the papers about those Jamaicans coming to Britain in 1948, but by the time the second and third boatload of West

Aylmer Beust instructing Leslie Thompson at London's Guildhall School of Music and Drama, *ca.* 1948

Indians came there was more fuss. I met a Miss Foster, through my Christian faith, who had been running a fellowship for flower sellers. In those days there were old ladies who sold flowers in Piccadilly and along Whitehall, and people like Miss Foster had realised that they should receive some kind attention. Not to interfere, but to offer support and assistance. The same way that organisations such as the YMCA and the Salvation Army had been assisting the poor and badly educated of Britain. She had a centre for them behind the Old Vic in the Cut, near Waterloo station. She and I discovered that a Jamaican fellow – a West Indian, certainly – had been helping these early immigrants. He was a minister; I can't recall his name. He organised meetings for these newcomers, and we went along. There was no fixed place, but each month the next meeting would be announced, and the word got about. We borrowed a hall from one church, and then another, all over south London, around Clapham and Brixton in the main. After a while he went to America, and Miss Foster and I carried on, aided by a West Indian student. This fellow was studying cabinet making, but he had to go back to Jamaica. We were doing this, after I finished musical work – so that would be 1954 – right up to 1960, making the West Indians feel at home and giving them some security of contact and faith.

After the war the Labour Party got into power, with a landslide victory, to make changes in peace of the magnitude that the war years had brought. But my socialist education was furthered, and my desire for my own personal progress reduced, by Oscar Rowe. He was a young Jamaican who had joined up in the West Indies and had come to Britain to be trained during the war. He was training in dentistry in the RAF when the war ended, and the authorities wanted to ship him back to Kingston and discharge him there. He was a dental mechanic, and wanted to study here, so I told him to stand firm, and he did, and was demobbed here. I met Oscar Rowe in Piccadilly at the end of the war, and we got to know each other well. When I was living in that big flat in Maida Vale he came to stay there, and so we shared for about two years. When I first met him he knew nobody, had no contacts here, but over the years he got to meet a lot of people. He was twenty-five or thirty years younger than me, and we would discuss things and he would say 'Mr Thompson – you're way behind the times.' In our talks he spoke of other places in the world, where whites kept black people down – places like South Africa and so on. When I said that white people wouldn't do that – not the English – he told me to read a book. I didn't believe him when he spoke of the pass laws, and the other indignities that Africans meet daily in their homeland, for I had heard of them but they were of no significance to me. So he handed me this book, *Britain's Third Empire*, by Padmore. When I read it that broke the bonds and I was converted.

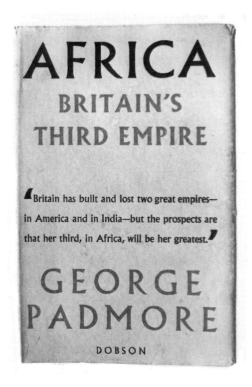

Dust jacket of
Padmore's *Africa:
Britain's Third
Empire*

I read a shorter book by Padmore, but I never met the man.
That book, *Britain's Third Empire*,[5] made me realise what it
meant to have a black face. Oscar was very keen and argued for
hours, and I called him 'the angry young man' after Osborne's
play that was in London at that time, around 1952. In a small
but important way those talks and that book of Padmore's
influenced my decision to give up making music for a living, for
my work was satisfying to me alone. I got the kudos from the
smiles of the dancers and the guests, but it wasn't of true value.
And the book also made me realise that universality is impossible if people are treated in different ways. Padmore's book
made me sit up with a start, and made me decide which course
to take. It was in his book that I read that in South Africa

African people could not go where they wanted, and that they had to carry a pass. The pass laws – it went through me like a rapier – I thought, my God – that you can't move without a document.

I stopped playing for a living in 1954, not because my dancing princess had become the Queen, but because I was getting to the point where I didn't see any reason to work those unsocial hours, starting at eight and playing up to six the next morning, when the dawn was breaking. I really and truly had had enough. Indeed the money was good, but I had saved something up, so I looked around. Eventually I managed to get a job as the warden of a residential home or hostel for under-graduates – off the bandstand and into the Alliance Club. This was run by the Evangelical Alliance for students in London, mainly at the university, and had started because of the prob-lems experienced by students from overseas. Many of the peo-ple in the movement had experience of Africa, especially of East Africa, and this time there was the Mau Mau. English landladies were slamming doors in the faces of Africans in London, and something had to be done. So these evangelical people, with their missionary background and faith, set up the Alliance Club in Bedford Place, and there we had eighty-odd students. I was there for nine years, until 1963.

5

Warden

The plan behind the Alliance Club was to have white students too, so that the overseas students had contacts with the natives of Britain. Many of these English fellows were the sons of missionaries with African experience, so they knew something of the background of the overseas fellows. One of the students, an African, is a Harley Street specialist today. One English lad lectured in maths at University College before he was twenty-one; he married a Jamaican girl – a coloured girl.

In the 1950s the influx of West Indian immigrants brought out a lot of prejudice. The white people kept away from the 'niggers' and so most prejudice was under the counter. When boatloads of black people came the media started it, all that nonsense about 'polluting the race'. The migrants were a neglected lot. I hadn't been treated badly in England, and in the 1950s I was distant from the newcomers, or from their fate, because I had a job, I had people who knew me, and I had a settled way of life. But when I stepped out of my area it changed. So I was made aware, from that, and from the West Indian fellowship meetings, that these poor fellows and girls from Jamaica, and elsewhere in the West Indies, were having a rough time.

They were exploited by black and white. They took any job, as I've said, and became bus conductors, street cleaners, any sort of job that whites didn't want, which didn't do much good as far as the natives were concerned, for they thought that all West Indians had no education, you know. I heard about the race riots in Notting Hill in 1958, and it was the same with the Brixton riots in 1981 and Tottenham in 1985.

Of course the students at the Alliance Club were likely to be affected by the now more open hostility of the English people towards coloured people, but I think even this was small because these students were really hard-working. And that hard work paid off, for there were many who have attained important positions and are leaders of their people. I'm not sure who I met through my work as warden, and who I met in other ways, but I do know that Festo Kivengere of Uganda, who was studying for the Institute of Education examinations when I was warden, became an influential churchman in Uganda. Indeed, I was able to meet Festo in Kampala only a few days before he escaped after his archbishop was murdered by Idi Amin. There was an Indonesian fellow whose name I have often seen in the news, concerning politics. A lot of these students became professionals: accountants, doctors, lawyers, and architects. Especially the people from Malaya; they became surgeons, barristers, and I can recall two who became chartered accountants. And politicians.

After the war, with the independence of India, Pakistan, Ceylon, and Burma, there was an influx of students. This swell was encouraged by the restrictions of the war years, which had reduced the numbers of students who could travel to Britain. It's a pity that Harold Moody died at that time, in 1947, for these new arrivals were an impressive lot. I didn't go to Dr Moody's funeral, but I knew that he had died. I can't remember how I learnt that, as I seldom bought a newspaper.

The richest British colony in tropical Africa was the Gold Coast, and it became independent, as Ghana, in 1957. As each

Alliance Club members – students from Africa and South Asia – at a wedding in Essex, *ca.* 1957. Leslie Thompson is third from the right.

new nation got its freedom I thought something good had happened. Actually, I am a great believer in Biblical prophecy, and, at the beginning of the Bible there is the story of Jacob. He was the grandson of Abraham, who had twelve sons. You will know that one son was sold into Egypt. Well, Joseph had two sons in Egypt – in exile. When the old man was 130, he met his two little grandsons. He crossed his arms when blessing them, placing his right hand, which was for the elder boy, on the head of the younger. That younger lad was to be a commonwealth of nations, so Jacob said. And I believe that it is coming true, for the United States was the elder son, and the Americans have become great, as the Bible says. And Africa and African people are new: adopted into the family of Abraham. I never met Kwame Nkrumah, who led his people to independence, nor did I meet Dr Clarke, the doctor in south London who was such a friend of Ghana and Nkrumah, but I

had heard of both men. Clarke had been associated with
Harold Moody and that pre-war group, the League of Coloured
Peoples, in London.

In 1956 Louis Armstrong came back to England. This time
he really had an all-star band, not a bunch of local lads. I went
to see him at the Empress Hall in London. I hadn't seen him
since we had said goodbye in France in 1935, so I got a couple
of tickets and went along. Actually I hadn't got anyone to go
with, but I saw a little West Indian girl near the show and she
told me that she was shopping for her mother; I said I would
take her in to see Louis and the All Stars if she had permission
from her mother. She rushed off and was back in five minutes.
We were quite close to the band. Louis had been so popular
that they had to form a guard to make a corridor from the stage
to the dressing room, in case he was mobbed again. I saw this,
but when the lights came on at the end of the concert and the
audience got up to go, I stayed in my seat. My little friend went
off: I told her to go. I wanted to see Louis, but there wasn't
any point in rushing, because I knew that his routine took
eight or ten minutes – peeling off his stage clothes, and being
sponged down, and then cooling off – that's why there are so
many photographs of him in his dressing room, for the fans
took them when he was just getting relaxed after the performance. After a while I got up and went along, and argued with
the commissionaires who didn't believe me when I said that I
was one of Louis Armstrong's trumpeters, of course. And out
came a coloured chap, Louis' dresser, and I said to him 'Will
you just go and tell Louis that his trumpet player, Leslie
Thompson, wants to see him?' My face was the right colour, so
off he went and Louis said yes – to the amazement of the commissionaires, of course. We had a good old chinwag about the
old days. I've got the programme which he signed 'To my ol pal
an trumpet man, Leslie – Satchmo Louis Armstrong'.

Ten years later, in 1966, I was in New York, but I never got round to seeing Louis, which I now regret. But in 1956 at the Empress Hall he was still playing with that force, hitting those top Fs. I saw that he was still the same as in 1934. He had that spontaneity of the good jazz player, and this was encouraged by the All Stars. His playing was so recognisable. Phrases you had heard before sounded as if they had been played for the first time, such was the man's genius. He was excellent. But he paid for this high standard with his life, because he had been so good so early that keeping up with his own standards was difficult, and there was the pressure of the younger men in America. An unforgettable man and a genius in music. The world will never be the same, because of Louis Armstrong.

It was in the 1950s that I bumped into Jack London's wife, in Southampton Row I think. She was English, and had married Jack in the early 1930s, but the marriage didn't last into the war years. It didn't last long at all, for she was a butterfly. She told me that Jack had died. I hadn't seen him since the late thirties when he, too, was running a club in London. It wasn't very successful at the time I visited it. That reminds me that I was out with Jack's sister-in-law – she had married a lad from Ceylon – in 1931, when we were working in *Cavalcade*. I was with them and [their daughter] Jack's niece, and we were driving past the Welsh Harp, in north London. We saw an estate being built. In those days the evening papers were full of pages – three or more – advertising houses for sale. We parked the car and had a look at the show house. Two reception rooms, either side of the front door; four bedrooms, a bathroom, a back room, kitchen, and a garage. The chap, a workman, made us welcome, and when we asked how much he said we should see the office. It was £1,000. In 1931 that seemed a lot of money, and – I was married then – when I told my wife she said 'forget it.' I really regret not taking it: looking back on it, I do wish I had bought that house up in Hendon.

At the Alliance Club the students would stay up to three years. The medical students eventually moved into hospitals, as resident medical men, but in their holidays they would come back. The idea behind the club worked, for the paint of anglicisation rubbed off on the students. They were also able to make contact with other educated coloured people, and in this way were able to discover elements in themselves, through these varied contacts, that made them throw off the cloak that had covered them back home. And in this way they were brought out, and saw life in Britain. I well remember one outing, on the upper reaches of the Thames, when we had a lovely day messing about on the river and having a picnic. I was in one boat, and to get to the bank I had to step onto the other boat which was tied up – and I missed my footing and went right in. Splash. And I had to go about half a mile before I could find a bush to change into a spare pair of shorts one of the lads had brought along: I had been soaked right up to my middle. There must have been other outings, informal affairs, when the students went, maybe four or five, on a bus or train, to Windsor, or the coast, and in that way they got about, got some fresh air, and became wiser.

In fact many of the students had been in Britain before they took up their studies, generally in the services but also as workers in the war industries, brought here during the war. The realities of English life, despite the problems, were such that life here was infinitely superior to life back home. How can I describe the difference? Here they could wear a collar and tie every day, not just on Sundays. They had seen that there were opportunities here in Britain, and returned to take advantage of them. Now, a generation later, the children of these migrants often have had the opportunity to 'go home' to the West Indies – taken back to their roots: but they don't fit there. Not only have the accents changed and mellowed, but the influence of

England, on all of us – all of us – has been so considerable that they would have to readjust to West Indian life. I went to Jamaica in 1980, so I speak from experience.

Just as I was thrilled as each African nation got its freedom, I am thrilled by the black people who are getting on here: authors, playwrights, television announcers, appearing in advertisements, and so on. When I came here the only time a coloured person was mentioned in the press was when there had been a crime. Yes, there has been a great deal of progress. You can see the result of education and experience. Some of the Jamaicans who came in the early 1950s were upset because they didn't get jobs in the same line as back home, but a nurse in Jamaica is not always someone who has studied in a hospital for three years, worked at her books and charts, and alongside doctors and specialists. A nurse in the West Indies was often a woman who could fix sprains, or be handy when a baby was expected, and that sort of old-style work. No wonder they couldn't get work here. You know that for centuries Britain, a British influence, has gone all round the world. This island has been a centrepiece in world history. Even in the far distant backwoods you will find a British influence. That attracts people here, and here all these particles of humanity will come together.

Just think of the Alliance Club in the 1950s, with twenty percent from Africa, and Indians, Chinese, Malayans, and English, and even some Americans and a couple of Australians. There were a few from France, just a few; but there were Swiss, Austrian, and German boys and girls – mainly language students – and these Europeans worked at the Club, cleaning and cooking, doing the housework – for the coloured students. Such a different atmosphere to the Jamaica of my youth.

The students were very serious. We had films or a talk of a Saturday night, and the occasional outing, but they buckled down to their studies. The greatest problem was financial. Can

you imagine the African or Indian parents, perhaps almost illit-
erate? They had come to the realisation that education was the
key to success, and through hard work gathered the lump sum
to finance the son's journey to London. But there was no more
when it ran out. The parents wouldn't have any more until the
harvest was sold, or perhaps they lived miles from a post office,
and it would take weeks for a letter to get to them: and then
they might have to wait to have a friend read it to them. And
this problem became my problem, for how could we tell them
to leave the Club because they couldn't pay the rent? One fellow, from Ghana or Nigeria came with the proper introduction
from someone who had stayed at the Alliance Club before, and
he paid seven months in advance. After that time was up, for
three weeks nothing happened. It got to nine weeks, and still
no money, so I wondered about it all; how could his parents let
him down? He came to me and said that he had to leave as he
hadn't got any money, and so he went off with a friend. Well,
when I later discovered that money had just been received
from his parents, I realised that his friend was not giving him
his new accommodation. That was the last straw for me. Mind
you, it wasn't my money, but the organisation's, and they were
sympathetic.

The eighty students had a choice of accommodation. Single
rooms were the most expensive, at £4–10s [£4.50] to £5 but if
you shared it was £4. And those who had two room mates paid
three guineas [£3.15]. This included breakfast and an evening
meal, and full board at weekends. As far as I know only a handful did not complete their studies, and just a few were not
successful at their examinations. But the majority were deadly
serious and completed all the work, and qualified: perhaps
some sat two or three times, but they swotted and, finally,
got through. Some came back as postgraduate students, and
some came back to settle and work in England. Mainly Chinese

fellows from Malaya, and a couple of Indians. One African doctor went to Ghana, where he had an excellent job heading a medical school. His wife – they had married here, when she was a nursing sister in London – had a responsible job out there, too, and all went well until the Rawlings coup around 1980, when they came back, with their three children. They told me that they were getting £100 a month in 1980, so how could they stay? And the political scene was unsettled, so they came back to London and have done very well since.

I haven't got too many details of what happened to everyone after they left the Alliance Club, but when I see one of them, fresh stories come to me about the careers of others. Dr Graham Gladwell, a brilliant mathematician who married a West Indian girl; four medical chaps – Dr Tom Anderson who went to Uganda in the 1960s, Dr John Carey, Dr John Beale, and Dr Felix Konotui Ahulu, are some names that spring up. Felix is an expert on sickle cell anaemia.[1] And there were two brothers, Raymond and Norman Skinner. Raymond was a brilliant teacher and worked in Devon, and his brother became a minister and is in Bideford. And three brothers named Kuok, too.

In late 1960 I was transferred to Brighton, where another fellowship set up the same sort of club as they had seen at the Alliance. The Brighton students were mainly at the polytechnic. The club was on Marine Parade, overlooking the sea. Local businessmen in the church supported it, but it didn't have that basis of English students to create the atmosphere of comradeship that the Alliance Club had, as there were mainly overseas students in Brighton – forty or fifty residents, the same mixture of Africans, Asians, and so on. It was a good mixture, but the atmosphere of such places depends so much on the people. Friendship House in Brighton was my responsibility for about a year, and in 1961 I returned to the Alliance.

The West Indian migrants of the 1950s changed Britain. I can well remember speaking at a men's forum, in the north west suburbs of London, on the colour bar, and I suggested that it was a question of one's personal view. We breathe the same air, but in the minds of some of us we write some people off, and exalt others. I am one of those who has been written off. Like me, these West Indian migrants are seeking to be re-established. I told this group that their children would not think the same way, and the little white ones will mix around with the little black ones. I said, 'Your daughter will be bringing a black friend home,' and this old man said, 'Never – never.' I was right, you know. Even at the Alliance Club, in the 1950s, when one of the white fellows married a Jamaican, I remember his mother at the wedding, and she said to me that her son was always a very determined young man.

As well as outings and social events with the students, and my church work, and the odd spot of music, I did travel. I had been to the Riviera – to the fashionable resorts of Cannes and St Remo, and to Venice too, in the late 1940s. I had a British passport then. And I went to Oberammergau in 1960. The passion play is put on every ten years, a timeless reminder of the village's oath which they made to God when asking centuries before, to be spared from the plague. I went on my own, but I sort of teamed up with a group from Wales, whose minister I had met somewhere before. There was a eucharistic congress in Munich, and I went to that for a day on my way to the passion play. We travelled by train. I would have been living in Brighton at that time, of course.

I left the Alliance Club in 1963, unsure what I was going to do. I did a couple of years there after the months in Brighton, and I looked round for another position as a warden. I phoned in response to a job advertised in the paper but the chap told me it was for a married couple; he suggested that London

University might have vacancies as they had lots of residential buildings in and around London. All those students – hundreds and thousands of them. So I got in touch with the Registrar who told me that they had no vacancies. He added, when he had heard my experience, that I should consider applying for work in the social services. There was the child care department, the adult welfare department, and the probation service. The people in the child and adult welfare sections told me that I would have to study for two years, and as I thought that I was a little too young to start studying – I was sixty-odd – I went for the probation service.

6

Probation and Prison

The probation office was looking for people. In fact, the newspapers were full of job vacancies of all sorts in the 1960s. So in 1963 I got in contact with a Miss Braithwaite, and I had an interview at the Home Office. The Home Office is at the Parliament Square end of Whitehall, and it doesn't look very big from the street, possibly because we're all checking the time by Big Ben. In actual fact it is very large, as I found out when I went for my interview. The chap at the door phoned up to check that Leslie Anthony Joseph Thompson, a Jamaican, was expected. And in I went, escorted by some flunkey, up a marble staircase. Then another chap took me along a corridor and up some more stairs. The building is hollow, like a cloister in an old church, or the quads in universities. So I walked along with my escort, along the polished corridor with the windows on one side and door after door on the other. I don't recall the number of flights of stairs, or the number of corridors, or the number of flunkies, but eventually I was passed to some official who took me up to a door, told me to wait, knocked, and went in. A moment later he came out and said that I should go in. And so I stepped in. A huge room with an acre of carpet and, in the distance, a table with a group of gentlemen and, I think, one lady. I recalled my West India Regiment days and the training, so I walked over smartly, across the carpet, stood with my thumbs to the seams of my trousers, looked at them all straight in the eye, and wished them good morning. Well, I had to answer questions on all manner of subjects for an hour, and that was that. But I got in.

In that way I joined the probation service in London. I continued to live at the Alliance Club until I got a place in Finsbury Park, although I put my name down for council accommodation. Bureaucracy takes time: I did look over a room, with a tiny cooking area. So I lived in north London until 1963 when I moved to Gower Street. I was able to get to the North London Magistrates' Court in Islington without too many problems, and I could get to my customers all over north London, too. It was quite extraordinary that I had no formal training. I had been quizzed for an hour at the interview, and I suppose they knew what they were doing.

Some of the staff at the court had heard that I was coming, and some of them looked a bit askance, thinking, no doubt, what's he going to do? Others were friendly from the very first minute; nobody was rude to me. My training was entirely practical; I had to see it all in action. So I was put at different tasks to see how it was done at the magistrates' court. I don't know if there was a deliberate policy to recruit coloured probation officers; certainly there was a shortage of probation officers, and that's why I think I got the job. I believe that the fellow who wrote *To Sir, with Love*[1] had been a probation officer in England, so I wasn't the first.

We took on whatever turned up. Some of the magistrates were fine; Mr Evelyn and Mr Milton, who both became senior stipendiary magistrates at Bow Street later on, were very nice to me. Even the policemen at the court were nice: they had a good look at me, but I passed their test. We had to deal with all sorts of people – young and old, men and women, drunks, intellectuals, the lot. The hours were from nine until four, with some nights. We worked in the locality. Sometimes the people would report to us, and we had to chat to see how they were getting on, and check that they were not misbehaving. And I had to visit their homes, generally in the evening. There was a pool of cars and you put your name down and off you would go. There wasn't any trouble over colour. 'Probation Officer' was enough. Of course the families were a bit careful, for I was an officer of the law. No uniform, but with the authority of the magistrates behind me.

There were some West Indians on probation, and their families were a bit friendly. I remember one family from British Guiana. The chap on probation had been a policeman back home, and here he worked as a driver. Stuff vanished, and the drivers were suspected, so they laid a trap, and caught quite a few; he was one of the first to be caught. Due to his service in Georgetown and his good reputation here, the chap was put on probation and was not sent to prison for theft. His wife was a nurse, they had three children, and the wife's mother was here, too. They lived in Dalston and I was always made most welcome there, so my visits were more social than official.

Most of the charges were like that: basically decent chaps who had been tempted. If they had been sent to prison their families would have really been in difficulties. Most of my contacts were white, but there were blacks, too. Foolish little crimes, like stealing a motor car, breaking into a gas meter, or breaking and entering. My first case was a coloured boy who had broken into the gas meter in his own home. I told him that this was stupid because the authorities immediately suspect someone inside the house and they would know that money had been taken. Young lads who just didn't think – they were my customers. I saw Learie Constantine once, in court. He had given up his cricket career and studied law, and was, at this time, the defending barrister. I had to stay in the court, but our eyes met. I have his book *Colour Bar*. I never spoke to him; I just never got the chance.

Our office was on the opposite side of the street to the court. There was a West Indian fellow who had a shop nearby, a real Jamaican shop, with fruit next to the soap, and things piled up in no real order. Anyway, normally we were all at work by ten o'clock, when the court was going. Our charges occupied our evenings, because they were usually at work in the day, and I was kept pretty busy. I lived at the Alliance Club for a time, and then I moved to a flat in Bloomsbury, but I didn't have much of a chance to do a lot as I was out until nine at night quite often. I was in the probation service from 1963 until 1971, officially retiring when I was seventy, but actually I kept on going. I had transferred to the prison service, as an officer in the probation and welfare section. After my official retirement I continued at the prison, at Pentonville, from 1971 until 1976, so even then, over seventy, I did some work at the prison until I was seventy-six. By that time it was just a few hours a day, in the educational department, teaching music. Anyway, in 1966 I went to America as a member of a trio. I took three weeks off and flew to Chicago, where I arrived on 9 August.

I had ceased earning a living at music in 1954, but I kept playing, and I found it useful in the Christian work which developed. Music is a great breaker-down of barriers, and so it was that I played my trumpet with a school teacher from the prestigious Westminster School, and a singer from Sri Lanka, Edward Thrumali – he changed [his name] to Eddie James. We three were the guests of American churches, and we stayed in the homes of church members. It was in the home of a negro millionaire, the Reverend John Cobb, that we lived in Chicago. He lived in a lovely house, one of those old time houses which had been built around 1890. A rich man's mansion. Whites had either left the area for the suburbs, or to the lakefront, a recent housing development in Chicago. Cobb even had his name in the pavement outside his home. I have no idea where he got his money. After Chicago we went to Detroit, and there we went round the huge Ford motor car plant. We travelled and stayed in various places in the state of Michigan, and then went to New York.

We spent a week in Brooklyn, with the Reverend David Wilkerson, who had written *The Cross and the Switchblade* in 1964; he is the original of one of the characters in *West Side Story*. Wilkerson had lived in the country, where he read in the newspaper about a drug addict in New York and the way in which these people had no hope in the big city. So he went off to New York, to work amongst the addicts. He was a real country yokel, and he had a rough time, from the addicts and from the police, too: he was ridiculed. Everybody made fun of him. Wilkerson would speak up for the addicts, and eventually the judges realised that he was sincere, but inexperienced. They and others helped, and he began to win the addicts over. He had a basement church in Greenwich Village, and he got Christian lads to go out amongst the addicts. When we were there his centre was in Brooklyn. He also had a farm, where the lads, usually city lads, could lead an open air life. I stayed in Brooklyn for a week. It was very uplifting.

This sort of work is alien to the sophisticated world – God intervening to change a man's life. Gradually, through the influences of others, a man would be turned. Gradually, gently. And our contacts on this American trip were all such people. In the end we played in twenty-nine churches; the singer, Eddie, never came back. He went off to Texas in 1966, and he's still there, although he goes to Sri Lanka, stopping in England, from time to time. He came here for open heart surgery. He had a heart attack in America, and he came here for a vital operation, but he had been away from Britain for so long that he didn't qualify for free medical treatment anymore. And so he went back to America, where the message went out – 'a new heart for Eddie' – and a collection gathered more than enough for the operation. The surgeon told him that he should have been dead long ago. Eddie was back on the road three months later, and he still is.

After this really exciting and stimulating time in America I got back to London on 30 August 1966 and continued in the probation service. I transferred to Pentonville prison, in north London, which is a prison specialising in drunks, prisoners on remand, and those who are serving up to six months. The Scrubs [Wormwood Scrubs] and Wandsworth, the other large prisons in London, were for longer-term prisoners. Life in prison is demoralising, absolutely hopeless. I have come to the conclusion, which is based on more than ten years working in the business, as it were, that prison is no place to reform people. In fact it is a breeding ground, a nursery bed – for good things and for bad things. Anything will be found in a prison. There were the down-and-outs, the derelicts, who were in their fifties and sixties. They went into prison for the winter, when life in the gutters of London was too hard. They got themselves arrested, and had three meals a day and a warm bed for the winter; and they had their pals – some of them knew everybody, rather like at a guest house with old residents.

Then there were the youngsters, who had been arrested for some crime, nothing too serious, often the result of bravado, and they would be in for three months. The prison system encourages prisoners to go along with the rules as all prisoners get one-third off their time for good conduct. Most of the Pentonville inmates were not the hard men, or people who were violent. They needed help, and it was my job to consider the welfare of the men. I had various colleagues doing the same thing. We had a wing each: four floors, with two to three hundred men. There could be all sorts of problems: a letter from home, from a wife or girlfriend, or a relative, who was upset, and this in turn would upset the prisoner, who would request to see the welfare officer. If it was my wing I would go to see the fellow, and I had to get to the root of the problem. I had to contact the local probation officer and get them to see the family to get the other end sorted out, too.

After a while there were a couple of coloured prison officers, but when I started I was an object of much interest and curiosity. Prison officers have a certain mental streak, which is based on insecurity. They seek to assert an aggressive attitude, especially to coloured people, the way it is today with some police. These lads were an odd mixture, mostly in their thirties. If your face was black they wanted you to show you were afraid of them: it was their way of receiving respect. Some police were the same, at Dalston and Islington at that time, and in Brixton today I suppose.

In the court at times, and especially if there were no witnesses, the magistrate would prefer to accept the prosecutions' word rather than the defendants'. By and large the system was fair, but some individuals weren't. I'll never forget one incident. This coloured fellow was in the court for a driving offence and was sentenced: his licence was taken away for a year or two. Our office was across the street, and his car was parked outside; in the 1960s there weren't any parking wardens, you see. He came out of the court, got into the car, sat in the driver's seat, and held his head in his hands. He was depressed; maybe he had to earn his living by driving. Anyway I was crossing the road, when two policemen came out of the court. They saw him – and they grabbed him. They took him into the court, and – how they got round the clerical system I still don't know – but they took him back before the very same magistrate, charged with driving without a licence. As if he was about to

drive off. He told the magistrate that he was waiting for someone to come – the poor fellow was shouted at 'How dare you.'
I was so angry but I couldn't do anything about it. I could stand
up and say 'These officers are telling a lie,' but that would cause
a problem between the police and the probation service, with
all sorts of effects for the charges of the probation officers.
And the police outnumbered me. And I was black. There were
two police officers – the poor fellow didn't have a ghost of
a chance.

On the other hand there were lots of decent fellows. At the
court there were the gaolers, who had to guard the prisoner at
the bar. They would bring the chap up, and in the courtroom
these two men stood there, guarding the prisoner as the case
went on. They were very decent fellows, who regarded it as just
a job. They would come to work wearing civilian clothes and
put their uniform jackets on in the office.

In the 1960s the drug scene in London was not like today. In
the 1950s a lot of musicians were experimenting with drugs,
which is how my son got involved; and this remained largely
true into the 1960s. And when I was in the prison service I met
the sons of my old band colleagues; one white and one black.
Just gone astray; so sad that it couldn't be corrected.

In 1966, my first year at Pentonville, I was walking along
when I met the governor, who asked if I would help at the
prison concert that Christmas. I had never spoken to him
before, but I knew him, and when we met face to face he asked
for my assistance, and in that way I was involved in music
again. There were some pretty good players in the prison, all
prisoners, all of them on drug charges. All of them were at least
semi-professional and a whole lot better than the bunch at
Devizes in 1942. So we got it together and had a jazz band for
the prison concert. The usual thing was to have three performances. The first would be for half of the inmates and the others

would be the audience for the second performance. And the final show was for an audience of staff, their relatives and friends, and the prison visitors. So our rehearsed jazz band of delinquents led by a Jamaican, yours truly, was pretty good by the third night, and impressed the head of the education department who came up to me and said that he hadn't realised that a man like me was in the prison. And he asked me if I would like to teach. He couldn't get anybody. Now I added a couple of hours, from six to eight or maybe nine, each night, to my work as a probation worker in Pentonville. And when my time was up in 1971 I gave up the probation side but kept on with the prison education department and there I remained until 1977. I can really say I've been to prison.

Because of those years I still get the odd tap on my shoulder, in the street, and some youngish fellow will ask 'Do you remember me?' And it will be someone from the prison. It is very moving when these fellows identify themselves in this way, because I feel it shows that my time wasn't all wasted, after all.

7

Tony

Despite all the pleasantries of my life a cloud came, and that cloud was my son. For a time he called himself Chris, but I always called him Tony, for he was Anthony Christopher Thompson. I had married in 1933 and Tony was born in 1937. Not very long after that my wife and I split up. There was the usual legal business, as it had to be in those days, something to do with desertion, but she had walked out and left us. Our divorce was completed by the beginning of the war, and, with the threat of bombing and invasion, I welcomed Kitty Marum's offer to take Tony to Ireland. Lots of London children went off to the country when the war broke out, and these evacuees also were sent to Canada, and all over the place, because it seemed so likely that there would be terrible devastation. Seen in that light Tony's years in Ireland were a good idea. For Tony it was a dream, because Kitty was a dear, and they got on so well together. So the little coloured chap had a ball of a time in Ireland with Kitty and her relatives and friends.

My wife had grown to dislike my late nights, for marriage to a musician is not one with a normal routine. Anyway, she went off with this engineer fellow, who was a northcountryman. He had his own business but, like so many self-made men, he was concerned that his background was so plain and ordinary. I met him a couple of times. Once, during the war, I met him at the

Shakespeare opposite Victoria Station, and he was in his full uniform, complete with revolver and webbing: a major in the Home Guard. And that pub was full of fellows in civilian clothes, enjoying a bit of leave from the services: how they looked at him. The poor chap died. He [had] married my ex-wife, but the marriage ended round about 1944. I was at Bickley, in Kent, and I went to see her then. In the 1950s, when I was at the Alliance Club, she came in, and for a few months things were affable. That ended, and it has stayed that way ever since.

Tony came to live with me in that large flat in Maida Vale, in Clifton Gardens, after the war, around 1950. When he was living in Norfolk he had joined the Sheringham brass band, and he had a few tips on music from me, and he messed about on my string bass. He worked in an optical business off Baker Street, and I suggested that he study lenses and optics, and got him into night school. Tony was about fourteen; Oscar Rowe was living with us, but Oscar had been in the airforce and they didn't have a lot in common. Tony had friends, and they would come to the flat when I was working, and there they would spend the evening, so Tony wasn't on his own. He didn't get into trouble until he was sixteen or seventeen, and in the army.

At night school he was to bone up on the theory and the engineering side of optics. And so he was out most nights. I would see him when he came in from work, but I had to go off to work, to Jermyn Street, and whenever I asked him how things were going it was the usual 'All right, Dad' of the young. I got concerned that there weren't any reports from the school, and eventually I phoned them, and I was told that Tony Thompson was a first class table tennis player. He didn't do any work there. So we talked it over, and I told him that you couldn't earn your bread and butter playing table tennis. He did another term, but there was no improvement: the headmaster confirmed that Tony Thompson was still a fine table tennis player. So I took Tony away, and put him in the army.

Years before, during those happy months at Kneller Hall, I had met lots of fellows and somehow we had kept in touch. In Jamaica we would hear from returning bandsmen from other regiments, and in other ways, what was happening to some of the crowd, and this continued after the regiment disbanded. I had this news, from the odd Christmas card and so on, in England, too. One of the students had been a fellow called Geary, and he and I with a chap called McBain who later was the director of music at Kneller Hall, studied under a chap named Jones who was studying to be a bandmaster. The system was that bandmasters, who had a more difficult course, had the bandsmen or instrumentalists under their wing. Jones had the three of us, back in 1920. Jones went on to be the director of music of the Royal Engineers. The other two went back to Kneller Hall and studied to be bandmasters, tutored by Adkins: and in this way Geary became a lieutenant colonel eventually. 6868 Thompson, later known as Bombardier Thompson, somehow kept informed of all this.

When Tony left the night school he was sixteen or so and I phoned Geary at Woolwich, to see if they would take him in the band of the Royal Artillery. McBain, by the way, had been put in charge of the music for the Household Cavalry and then took over at Kneller Hall. Well, Geary told me that he would be only too pleased to consider Tony, and we went along to Woolwich. Tony said he would play 'The Holy City' on his cornet, which led to groans – there had been six others playing the same tune, that very week. Well, his cornet playing was good enough and Tony joined the Royal Artillery band in, what – 1953.

There was another link to Kneller Hall, in Paddy Purcell. He was a great big Irishman who had won the medal there in

1919 and went on to study the clarinet at the Royal Academy of Music. He was bandmaster with his regiment in India and eventually became a civilian. I hadn't seen him since 1924 when his band had performed at Wembley. Thirty years later Paddy was running a boys' band, but was sort of semi-military. He came with Geary and myself to a pub and we talked about the old days, the swags, the medals, and this and that. Of course I was very pleased not only because Tony had the opportunity, but that there were senior people I could consider to be my friends, keeping an eye on him.

Tony changed from the cornet to the trombone, and took up the string bass as his second instrument. He had fiddled about on mine, so it wasn't strange for him. This wasn't the bass I had at Wembley, which I had purchased from the regiment in 1926 and brought to England in 1929 – I don't remember what happened to that fine instrument. Paddy's little lads played so well, and Tony's bass playing, with that swaying and acting that I had told him about, was remarked on – they played during the tea at an open day for parents at Woolwich and I remember the praise from people standing near me – and so Tony got to know local musicians. They called him out of an evening to play at this or that function, sometimes in central London, and often late at night. And this is how Tony got into the wrong company. Late nights and slack personal discipline led to poor work standards and so Tony was brought to the attention of the military authorities who planned to send him to one of those tough centres, where he would be sorted out by tougher standards. He didn't want to go, of course, as I well knew from his comments during his leave. It was pretty certain that he would be sent to this special training camp when he returned to Woolwich after his leave ended. I was away, but a friend phoned me to say that Tony had taken an overdose. He had gone to the old medicine chest and mixed up all the pills and tablets, a cocktail, and swallowed the lot. Then he walked to

Paddington hospital, said he had taken an overdose, and was pumped out and kept under observation. He was eighteen years old, or so, at this time.

He went back to the regiment but the Paddington hospital people sent a report, and the army doctor called me up. The tests showed that Tony was a hard drug user, and the army was no place for addicts. It was quite a shock to me. I had given up smoking, as I've said, and drinking was the odd social glass of sherry; when the chief medical officer told me that Tony was a drug addict I was shocked. Tony came out of the army and came back home. Then his real nature appeared. He would be out for days, never returning home unless he wanted something. He took my typewriter, a camera, and binoculars, and sold them for cash for fixes. He had links to pushers and those lads in the London music scene who he had first met when he was in Woolwich. He played both the string bass and the trombone; Chris Thompson was his professional name. It was the fashion in some jazz circles in the 1950s to experiment with drugs, and my Tony was pulled into that group.

At home there was no woman to look after him. We had a wonderful lady, Mrs Hughes, who cleaned and cooked. She was very kind. Tony had been with friends all his life, from those years in neutral Ireland when the rest of the world was at war, to Norfolk and Sussex, and in London with me. He was in the Sunday School, and he had many friends in the church. All my friends knew him, and he was not pushed out of our conversations. I can't see that he had no freedom. So he didn't burst out, as it were, and so get into the wrong company, reacting against parental discipline. He kept on with his church, too, right up to the time he joined the army. In the army there were lots of lads his age; an opportunity to study, learn, enjoy music and comradeship. He had the books I had had back in 1920 – those, and my trombone, I've never seen again.

You might think that, as a coloured lad in a white society, he had to fight to get an identity, and so he resorted to drugs to either keep down the pressures or to reflect the nastier side of life here, but I don't think that was true. We had black friends, not a great deal, but he wasn't isolated: Oscar Rowe; Dr Dele Alakija – he came here from Nigeria, for this and that, and usually stayed at our flat. He came over on a tropical medicine course and stayed with us for months. He and Lily had broken up shortly after they went to Nigeria. Actually he was the doctor who attended Tony's birth, so you have to agree that there was a lasting and warm friendship here. And Africans, of course, would pop in, or stay.

Besides, Tony was brought up in a white environment. All my years in England I had been cut off from the West Indians except that spell in the band in 1936 and 1937. None of us talked of 'home' and there wasn't that sort of thing, the cooking of ackee, peas and rice, a sort of Jamaica-in-England. I felt that Tony was fully integrated into English life. Perhaps it changed when he was a teenager. There was plenty of liberty – to play table tennis. Freedom? He wasn't interested. Oscar was closer to him in age, and there were two other Jamaicans who were around a lot at that time. One of them, a little fellow, you see from time to time in films. The other was also a singer, by the name of Johnny Lyon. He had a remarkable voice, for he was a male soprano. I met him in Jamaica in the 1920s, at a Christmas morning concert at Ward's. Wonderful. He came out of the blue. He came to England, and he would practise in my flat, for our piano was good, of course. Johnny Lyon had to perform a Handelian opera, in Camden, with Joan Sutherland who then had an international reputation. I recall him practising and how his voice was so remarkable. In Jamaica he had been a civil servant, but something went wrong and the blame was pinned on him so he resigned and came here around 1947. He was in our place two or three times a week.

Tony's group of friends included a closely knit group of children at the Westminster Chapel around Dr Martin Lloyd Jones, a wonderful man. One particular family there had a son named Sherman and he and Tony were close pals. I really do not think that parental influence had anything to do with Tony's decline – I mean, although I worked in the evenings, there was a parental influence. It was that casual evening work that he got into in the army and, through that, meeting those people. Men and women of good positions and from good homes – good people with excellent education too – get hooked on drugs. I saw it in Pentonville, you see. Had I called in the police when Tony walked off with my valuables it would have made no difference. You have to be changed from within.

Tony went to prison a number of times, in the late 1950s and the 1960s. One time he was in Wandsworth but I didn't see him there because I only found out about it much later on. The police fiddled matters, it seems, and stitched another charge on him, and his sentence was extended. Eventually a new psychiatric prison was opened at Grendon Underwood, near Bicester, out in the country towards Oxford. Tony was sent there, and I went there to see him two or three times. The treatment there worked, and Tony really changed. He edited the prison newspaper, and became a good runner. A lecturer at that prison and the probation officer in the welfare department supported Tony and got him released on parole. One of the conditions was that he must live miles away from London, where his old drug contacts were. He stayed at the flat and the next day went to Sheffield where he got a well-paid job in the steel mills. I had £200 saved for him, and I gave it to Tony so that he had something to start with.

One of the Grendon Underwood doctors kept in touch with Tony after he completed his two or three years at that prison, and got him to study. He went to night school in Sheffield, and eventually became interested in the idea of working for a mature scholarship. Someone suggested it to him, and he was one of about eight hundred who applied. He was short-listed, and got a place, one of thirty or forty places, and he went to Bristol University. I hadn't seen Tony for a long time, but I knew he was at Bristol and when, by chance, I switched on the radio and heard it was *University Challenge*, with Bristol versus some other place, I listened. There was a Tony Thompson in the team, but I wasn't sure until he spoke. It was Tony. He got the answer wrong, by the way.

So he was about thirty, and studying at Bristol University. He wasn't the Chris Thompson, musician and drug addict, of the earlier years, and I hoped he would settle down. I was living in Gower Street and working at the prison at this time, and he would come and stay with us during the vacations. Time went by and I didn't see him, and eventually I phoned the university, and they looked up their papers, and told me that Tony Thompson had failed the finals. He had taken social anthropology, a typical decision, for it's a tough subject. I had no idea where he was, or what he was doing.

I was working at the prison when I found out that Tony had died. Frankly, I hate to think what a mess he had got into. When I was at the Alliance in the 1950s I used to see Johnny Lyon, who worked in Holborn and would pop in when he had a moment. One morning he came in, and told me that he had seen Tony the night before – shoeless. He had Tony with him: I went out, took one look, and went back to my room where I filled a suitcase with clothes, which I took down to Tony. I gave him two pounds and told him to go to the public baths, take a bath, wear what fitted him from the suitcase, and get something to eat. I didn't see him for a long time after that – he never came back that day. Generally Johnny Lyon managed to find him when he surfaced from the depths of London, or somehow he found out where he was, and so I would get a message. Of course he sold everything he could get, for the next fix.

One day I got a telephone message from this lady, his probation officer, who had been looking after Tony following his latest criminal stupidity. It seems that, in view of his time and activities at Grendon Underwood and Bristol, the magistrate put him on probation, provided he stayed in Acton – or Ealing – it was west London. Tony was capable of being very charming and the people at the house and his probation officer let him go out, and he naturally ended up in central London and mixed with the same drug crowd. So, trusted by these people in Acton, he got back to searching for a fix. He died from an overdose of drugs.

The funeral was delayed until the afternoon of the day his probation officer got back from leave, and so she didn't know and that's why I had no idea that my son had died until the very day of the funeral. I got time off and went by car, passing a hearse at the side of a road, which turned out to be Tony's hearse, for I recognised it when I arrived at the church. Quite a fair amount of Tony's friends were there, in the church, but not too many went to the grave, for it was really pouring with rain, I'll never forget it. I sent the vicar £25 to offset some of the cost.

Some time later, I was teaching one particular prisoner the saxophone in Pentonville. He was in on a drug offence, or some act connected with drugs, and he asked me if I was Tony's father. He had been in the room when Tony came in, all lit up with drugs – spaced out, as the expression has it – and he was there when Tony died. He had seen my son die.

The wrong company – a victim of the terrible evil of drugs. Before that he was perfectly happy. I feel that – I don't like to think about it – I feel that it was a wasted life. He had the misfortune to be caught up in the drug-taking crowd. It can happen to anyone. I had to deal with it in the probation service. That prison jazz band was full of ex-addicts, for instance. It's hard to know what to say. Circumstances beyond one's control.

Each of us comes into the world alone; we live our lives; and our thinking and inclinations, and emotions, govern us. And, although we have the advice of parents, friends, loved ones, ultimately it is what we do that counts. In the case of a child, a loved one, who has become a victim of drug-taking, there is no one. We can try to help them, but ultimately they – that person – must exercise that something within them. They must say 'Enough' and call it a day. Until they do that, you and I are powerless. Personally, as a father, and as an adult of a little experience in life, I find that there is one avenue that one can take in this situation, and that is – perhaps – what the world will laugh and sneer at. And that is – take the matter to God. I say that. Some words have governed me.

'Be anxious for nothing but by prayer and supplication, with thanksgiving, make your requests known unto God.' For some, that prayer might seem trite and meaningless. For others it means everything. I am one of those.

A young life, thrown away like that. I've had a lot of experience with drug addicts. [Addiction] is evil. It is beyond the power of man himself to cope with. It can happen to anybody. And there is no easy solution. But rest assured, God has the solution and whosoever calls upon Him will be heard, and answered. Many, many converted addicts will confirm that – from their own experience.

8

Africa and Jamaica

I was still doing a few hours a week in Pentonville in 1976 when I went to Africa. I applied for a British passport: they took my old one, which had expired, and I never got it back. I was told to go to the Jamaican High Commission in Mayfair. In a way I was proud of that British passport. So I was a Jamaican after all my years in England; the best part of half a century.

It was due to the Alliance Club that I knew this fellow named Stephen. He studied hard and qualified as an accountant and he went off to Africa for two or three years and came back. He told me that I should go to Africa; indeed, his letters used to invite me, but I only agreed with him because that's what you do when people keep on at you. I thought no more about it. He went off again, to Nairobi, and came back, and again I got an invitation. I knew it wouldn't happen. Stephen went off, and one morning I got a letter – inside was my return ticket to Nairobi. I couldn't believe my eyes.

I went on my own. I left London on 22 December 1976 and arrived in Nairobi, the capital of Kenya, where Steve met me. He was married, and they had three children (they all live in Devon now). I stayed at his house in one of those lovely suburbs of Nairobi. I had extra leave from the prison, and was away about nine weeks. A lovely meal, a smashing house, and a long sleep after a very long flight. I was quite tired; but in the morning I was relaxed, no bother about what to wear, because you don't bother with such things in the tropics – overcoats, or jackets, and all that sort of thing. His house was where the elite had lived back in colonial times. He had two families as servants – I was in luxury. Stephen was in charge of his company's accounts, and went off to the office early, and so we seldom saw him in the course of a normal day. I lounged about on their verandah. I walked into the city centre, to have a look around, and to go to the post office, but I had been told to be careful, so I was always looking over my shoulder. When Steve had to go into the country I went with him in the car, and I also joined him and his family when he had to go to Tanzania, to Dar es Salaam. Stephen had to visit a fellow there so we stayed for a week. This would be from 9 January to 15 January 1977, according to the stamps in my passport.

We got back to Nairobi and after three weeks we went to Uganda. This looks close on the map, but it is a long drive. In those places no one thinks a lot before setting off on a car journey which here would take you to the north of Scotland or in Jamaica would – if you could swim – take you beyond the western part of Cuba. We went by the motor road up to the hills and across the Rift Valley, into Uganda, and then to Jinja. We drove over the dam there, where the Nile starts its journey into Egypt. I recall the sugar cane in this area and the drive into Kampala. There were three of us: Steve; a lad who lived in Kenya – an English lad; and me. We took a light plane to the north, to a game park. It was a five- or six-seater plane, and we got to the landing strip but there we got into difficulties. The airstrip was some distance from the lodge where we were booked in, but they didn't know anything about us and so there was no transport to meet us. Eventually someone got through to Kampala and explained, and they got through to the lodge, and someone came to collect us. We went out on the Nile to see the falls and the whole area was infested with crocodiles. One large one was on a sandbank, snoozing in the sun, and the boatman turned off the engine and we drifted towards the croc; one camera click and he was awake and – whoosh – gone! We saw a leopard, which is unusual, but no lions. There were lots of elephants and no end of hippos. There weren't a lot of people at the lodge, the hotel where we stayed, about twenty-five I think. All tourists, of course. We flew back to Kampala without any problems.

Steve had lived in Kampala before, and we stayed with one of his old friends, or rather at his house, for I never met the chap and I think he was away and let us have the run of his house. It was near Mengo, where the hospital is, quite close to the Anglican cathedral. In the morning I went to see the tomb of Bishop Hannington,[1] the early Christian missionary. I can well recall all the steps up to the cathedral – Namirembe, isn't it? A curate spotted me, and took me over to a corner where they had photographs of the early missionaries, all bearded, fierce-looking fellows, medical missionaries, too. So I saw the historical basis of the place; and I saw Bishop Hannington's grave.

We were getting ready to leave Kampala to return to Nairobi when Steve said he had to pop into town. He came back and said that we should leave as soon as possible, so we jumped into the car and were over the border, out of Uganda, before the news of the outbreak got out. I can't recall the name, but some disease had broken out in Kampala and if we had delayed we would have been refused entry into Kenya or placed in quarantine. In 1977 things in Uganda were not too good, for Idi Amin[2] had been running the place for five years and there wasn't a great deal of wealth or trained people. All the Asians had been expelled, and firms had closed down. The army was in charge.

Actually, on my first day in Kampala I went to a Christian fellowship meeting in a hotel in Kampala, and there I asked after Festo Kivengere from the Alliance Club. Of course they knew him and I was told that he was living on the campus at Makerere University; if I went up there, I was told, I would find out where to find him. So we went off, and eventually I was told he was at the archbishop's palace, where there was a conference. When we got to the conference I was told that I might be able to see Festo at four o'clock, at tea time. To fill in the time I went to see the Kabakas' tombs. The magnificent grass-thatched tomb of the old king was in an enclosure on the edges of Kampala. Back to the palace and there I saw Festo, for the first time in twenty years. He introduced me to all the bishops, including Archbishop Luwum. Only a few days later Festo, with another churchman, went with the Archbishop to Amin's place, and the pair waited in the car. A high-ranking army officer told them to leave before they were in the same position as Archbishop Luwum. And, as we all know, he had been murdered by Idi Amin. Festo escaped and got to England. The church authorities were beginning to be an alternative to Idi Amin's regime, and by murder and fear he put an end to that and kept his control of Uganda until he was overthrown.[3]

Although I was in East Africa for eight weeks – I got back to London on 22 February – I was a tourist, and I had no opportunity to discern the ethnic qualities of the people. I could see no great difference between the places, because we lived in the nice suburbs of major towns, travelled by car along the main roads, and saw developed farming from the roadside. Sugar cane, tea, coffee, and so on. The dam at Jinja was a wonderful bit of engineering. I was impressed by the style of the women in Uganda, because they dressed more typically African and looked very smart. Actually, I think I knew that Idi Amin had banned western dress, but those long dresses and

the short sleeves were very becoming and looked so right in
that setting.

One time in Kampala we went to a school where some of
Amin's children were boarded. The headmistress, who was
English, never took much notice of Idi Amin, who told them
what to do, but she and her staff were relieved when the
children went elsewhere. Then they felt safer. The children
didn't want to go, but the teachers were pleased to see the back
of them because of the threat that their father posed all the
time.

It is hard to assess my African trip. I felt that something was
missing; that development wasn't on a firm basis. But I was like
a tourist. Compared to Jamaica which I visited in 1980 – and
hadn't seen since 1929, remember – the buildings were very
advanced. In Jamaica, in 1980, the poverty in the lowlands was
terrible, and I got the feeling of inner frustration. It's hard to
describe. But when I walked along the street in Jamaica all the
faces looked at me: all those people on their doorsteps, looking
at the stranger walking by. But I didn't go to similar areas in
Africa, apart from a brief look with Stephen, when we went
near a shanty town in Nairobi. There were the zinc roofs, the
standpipes for water, and the open drainage: such a contrast to
the wealthy suburbs. But in Uganda and Kenya there is something, a more bountiful providence, that appeals to the eye.
Things look more prosperous – flowers, and colours, and also
the light which is so different to that of London. The people
were not at all unpleasant – they were in Jamaica – but, due to
Amin's regime, they were more serious in Uganda. I think the
Amin psychology had got to them. But everyone was helpful,
and that made the whole trip to East Africa such a very pleasant experience.

When I got back to London from Africa I arrived at
Heathrow, and there the signs had 'British passports' and I

went there, where I was asked to join the 'non-British' travellers. Of course I had a Jamaican passport. I was kept waiting for half an hour and, without any interview, they let me in. I suppose that I qualify, in some government statistic, as a Commonwealth immigrant who arrived in February 1977.

I was busy with this and that, and there wasn't anything special until the middle of 1980, when I went to Jamaica, for the first time since 1929. The flight out was quite interesting, because the passengers had so many different attitudes. It was an Air Jamaica flight, and there were all manner of people on it. Some were conversing, others were sleeping, yet others were having a party and those were laughing and talking. It was quite a mixed group. When I arrived in Jamaica I was quite surprised, for I got through the customs and suddenly someone called out 'Leslie, Leslie,' and I saw a fellow I had been to school with at Alpha – seventy years before. And there was one of the nuns, and a priest, who had a mini-bus: I felt like a VIP.

It was gone midnight, but the Reverend Mother at Alpha had waited up to talk to me. The Alpha School, started with such faith so long ago, was one hundred years old. I went on a tour of my old school after I had taken a good night's rest. I had left in 1917 to join the West India Regiment; it was the centenary year and I was part of the celebrations. I saw changes in the place that the years had brought. When I was there as a boy there was a bandroom and a shoe shop, where repairs and the making of shoes were learned. In the 1910s the rest of the activity went on in the fields, with the lads growing and weeding. And in 1980 there was printing, photography, tailoring, and lots more. But what hit me, smack – was when I went into this room where they had a list of names of the boys who had achieved, for the first name on that list was Leslie Thompson. I must confess that my eyes were filled with tears. The boys knew, and they looked at me. I couldn't believe it.

Later on I went to listen to the band practice. I had met the bandmaster a few hours earlier and when I walked in they played, especially for me. I felt very emotional. A little boy in the band, so long, long ago. And now, listening to it all as an old man. There was a concert, and the Mother Superior asked me if I wanted to conduct, but I wanted to keep a low profile. That concert hall was big, for it was for the boys who boarded, for the girls at the high school, and for the pupils at the day school. Half way through, at the interval, there was a presentation of some flowers, and I was asked to say a few words. Another time there was a concert at the boys' school, with an audience of parents and friends. They asked me to play, so I borrowed a trumpet and played Handel's 'Largo', an easy piece: after all, I hadn't played my trumpet for a long time.

Soon after I got to Jamaica I went for a walk, to look around, to see how the old place had changed. I went to Jones Pen, which somewhat grandly was now called Jones Town. I was walking there. Now that I am back in London, with hindsight, I can see that I did invite a certain sort of attitude. I had on a clean shirt, and a pair of trousers with a pressed crease. I didn't look the part. So those eyes looked at me, for anyone could see that I didn't belong to the spot. I stuck out a mile, I suppose. They mugged me. I don't feel angry, for they were doing what was done and I was asking for it. I invited it. I must confess that after that I didn't venture out on my own at all.

I was taken to Up Park Camp, and I saw it from the outside. I went in to hear the band – the Jamaican Military Band – and the bandmaster stopped them to tell them who I was. It was like that during the whole of my trip to Jamaica, from 31 July to 10 September 1980. A prodigal's return, you might say.

There were profound changes in Jamaica over that half century. There was a university, equivalent to a British university. Actually a terrible thing happened to me. I had met a chap named Cedric when I was in Hampshire visiting some friends, and I mentioned that I planned to visit Jamaica, whereupon Cedric told me that he was a warden at the university and that I should visit him when I was in Jamaica. He said that I should look him up when I got to Jamaica. I was on the campus a number of times, visiting and recording some items for broadcasting on the radio, and I completely forgot that invitation from Cedric. I was back in England, talking to those particular friends, when they said that Cedric's letters asked when I was coming. Then I realised – I had come and gone, and ignored the man. I haven't had a word from him and I have been too ashamed to write to apologise. How could I do it – just a simple and painful mistake.

At the university campus I met several intellectuals, and in Jamaica, indeed the whole of the West Indies, you have to show that you are somebody – that you have achieved a rank, or status. And one fellow did this by using long words. It is a very noticeable trait there. When people are left in such ignorance they react by stressing elements which, in a more adjusted society, are not so very important. That chap's book was written in that way, too. Here in England the door of opportunity is open – it is more open. Of course, compared to the Jamaica I had left, I could see that the door of opportunity was opened wider in 1980. But that almost overwhelming sense of ignorance is still strong; that's why West Indians stay in Britain.

There were terrible disadvantages in Jamaica. Here we have a bath, and a toilet indoors; in the country in Jamaica you have to cross the yard to go to the lavatory. Then energetic Jamaicans, who sought their opportunity in Panama and in New York, and in Britain after the war, may still not have a good opportunity in Jamaica. Of course the CIA and the political mess, and the economic situation – the throwing out of work of all those people – made life in Jamaica worse, but the real cause is colonisation. Slavery, and then colonisation.

For centuries, slavery and colonisation. The few years since the end of colonial rule in Jamaica are so very short to be able to change habits.

There is more elbow room for Jamaicans in Jamaica, but there is still that greater opportunity here in Britain. Today, so many coloured people are British, born here in Britain, that there will be better chances, bigger bites at the apple of British life in all its aspects. That economic yoke in Jamaica, in 1980, was still visible. When I was a child we were poor but we got by; in 1980 the CIA threw a whole nation out of work. And there was the killing and the violence, fed by people who had no interest in the future of Jamaica. It was so bad that I was afraid to go out. Poverty-stricken people, poor for so long, so easy to manipulate with promises and power.

That poverty of Jamaica, and the West Indies, is a special kind; there is an attitude of dependence. Even when nation-hood came, we who lived in England could see that the people in Whitehall and Westminster had the idea for posterity, so that it would look good and their names would be respected. In actual fact the knot was tied tighter. The pressure that had been in Jamaica when I was young was still there in 1980. A dependent state, unable to achieve without assistance. When you leave such a country there is a feeling that the shackles are falling away. The pressure changes so much that you can feel it. Yet, when you are there and if you never move away, that pressure is part of you, and you adapt to it, and get used to it. In 1929, when I left Jamaica for England, to try my future in Britain, I remember looking back across the ocean where Jamaica was out of sight below the horizon. In fact, I think it was on the second day out. Anyway, I had a sixpence, and I pulled it out of my pocket, and threw it towards Jamaica, and said goodbye. It was an act of liberation. Getting away from all that pressure.

In Jamaica we sang, laughed, and talked, and were used to
the pressure but that oppressive pressure is seen clearly, so very
clearly, when you leave. And here in England when the economic pressures have subsided, you feel that somehow you are away
from that. So the West Indians, despite all the drawbacks to
life in Britain, do not have that pressure. There are old-timers
who have driven their trains, cleaned the streets, collected the
bus fares, and so on, and now have a pension here. They know
that they have got above it; the pressure is off. Some might
want to return to the Caribbean, but – as happened with me –
it isn't clear. There isn't a simple answer. Why, a fellow I knew
in the regiment, who was living in the States when I was back
in Jamaica in 1980, wrote to me and said that we should both
settle back in Jamaica. He, apparently, had enough money and
his letter suggested that we could get together and settle in,
there. No – I couldn't go back.

All I have in Jamaica is a sister. When my mother died in
1935 I had a plot of land. A fellow suggested that, as I was in
England, I should sell it and turn it into cash, and he made me
an offer. I talked it over, and I said to myself that I wasn't going
back – this was in 1935 – and I sold that plot of land, and from
that moment in 1935 I had no roots in Jamaica. That land tied
me, and it was important, just as it is for Irish people here in
England, who had a plot back in the old country. When it was
sold the link was severed.

To uproot myself and settle in Jamaica is a difficult decision
even after half a century. Apart from the fact that I might need
medical attention here, as I'm not getting any younger, the
truth of the matter is that I am in an English setting, and have
been in an English setting for over fifty years. Although I'm a
transplanted West Indian, I will not make the mistake people
make when they retire. Having lived all their working lives in
one area, they uproot and move to the coast, and everything is

turned upside down when you sell up and move. You move away from your old contacts and it is years later before you realise how important they were. My West Indian influences have been minimised since the 1950s, and England has changed, and today black people can be seen doing things – doing this and that – which were almost unheard of in my early days here.

Of course it is difficult for black people here in England, but there are changes. The people who came here in the 1950s may be West Indian, but they have changed over the years, and their children are not West Indians, but English. I have lived so long in Britain that it is my home and I belong here. I am thankful that I had the opportunity to see Jamaica again, in 1980, but London is my home now.

Over and above the economics of life there is a spiritual fount which is vital to us all, whether we know it or not and that I've discovered in England. And it has made all the difference to my outlook. As a result I view the future with a great hope, which I know will be fulfilled. So I am, indeed, quite genuine in my desire to continue to make England my home, and to put myself at the disposal of my fellow mortals irrespective of race, colour, class or creed.

9

Reflections

There comes a time in the life of most of us when we pause along life's way, to take stock of ourselves. Maybe some circumstance or event has somehow affected the normal flow of our life and caused us to pause, and take a look at ourselves to see where and how we stand. That experience has occurred a few times in my life.

The first took place when I was in my middle twenties in Jamaica. I had borrowed a motor bike – a Canadian Red Indian – after just learning to ride one for the very first time. I took off along the coast road going east from the city. Soon the shops and houses were behind me so I decided to put the throttle full on and let her go. The joy of the breeze plus the excitement of tearing along at the then-enormous speed of eighty miles an hour caused the adrenalin in me to rise. In the midst of the enjoyment a goat, which had been feeding on the bank some distance ahead of me, decided to move, very leisurely, at right angles across my path. At that moment I knew that the goat and I were in for a meeting very soon. Somewhere within me something told me I might not be here after that meeting; suddenly my whole life – up to that moment – just unfolded before me in full detail. It all happened so fully, suddenly, and quickly that I even had time to think before I reached the goat. I decided to just ditch the bike – which I did

Leslie
Thompson,
November 1985,
(courtesy Jeffrey
Green)

by a sharp twist of the handlebars. I was still going very fast, but this brought the front wheel round and the machine came to a sudden stop. Because I'm alive to talk about it I can tell you that I now realise what a foolhardy action that was. But the impact of the engine simply broke the wheel guards and plunged into the earth, making an enormous hole, and causing me to just fall off backwards. I've never forgotten that experience. Others have come along since, when death looked me in the eye.

There was the time I was grabbed by a non-swimmer who was well out of her depth in the sea. She threw her whole weight on me and I was completely under the water, gasping for breath. I managed to snatch a lung-full of air and dived out of her grasp and she let go, but in her panic she grabbed at me again, and that grab left me stark naked. But I was able to escape being drowned. Again, before I was free I saw my life all over again. Another time I was a passenger in a car which was knocked over at a turn-off; and another time when my life came before me was when I was knocked off my bicycle by a car. These experiences I well remember but somehow they did not affect the course of my life.

The one event that did the trick was, at first, just an ordinary everyday experience of meeting new people. I had popped into a nightclub in the West End after work, and there I was introduced to a tall lanky young Guyanese student named Ken Johnson. He was studying languages at High Wycombe, Buckinghamshire. He seemed far more interested in the stage than in languages; he was a charming and vivacious person and we often met at odd places in the West End and, as a result, we came to know each other quite well. He confided in me that he really wanted to become a dancer, so I advised him to get together with American dancers who came to England on variety dates. After a while he packed up his studies and began to hang around the West End tagging on to theatrical folk. Then he went off to America for a while, where he made a close study of the stage acts there. On his return to London some months later I could see that he had picked up a couple of step dance routines, and one particular one, dancing up and down some stairs, which eventually became his *tour de force*.

Ken Johnson and I talked of all sorts of ideas until he suggested that I should form a coloured band, which should be a big hit in England at that time. I had suggested that he get with a band, but his idea was good, and I gave it some thought. He persisted with the idea, and so I agreed to go ahead, on the understanding that he would be the dancer, and dummy conductor, cutting capers and living up to the name – 'Snakehips'. He would be in front of the band. For me this was a change of direction. For the previous fifteen years I had grown to be one of the well-known players in the profession, and to lead a band now meant that I would have to abandon my connections in the theatrical world, and amongst serious musicians, and concentrate in stick wagging, which in front of a dance band even a child could do, given a little commonsense.

Ken didn't know any music but he could wiggle and waggle himself to the time of the music, and so keep onlookers amused and interested and I would be able to play. In order to avoid awkward queries about the band we always used a nameless title, like the Emperors of Jazz, or West Indian Swing, or some title that caught the public's fancy. We were fortunate around that time as four lads arrived from Jamaica, and their presence along with the local boys made it possible to get a good band on the road. To start a band from scratch one first of all has to have the appropriate means: cash. Cash for the hire of rehearsal rooms; cash to buy equipment; cash to pay for publicity and photographs; cash for music and arrangements; and perhaps the most expensive item – and one which was always present – uniforms or costumes. We needed cash for music stands; cash for amplification equipment; and more cash. The boys needed subs to keep them from starving in the first weeks, and we had to pay agents and management.

During the years I had been in England I had tried to be a bit careful with money, as I knew from bitter experience how suddenly economic changes can occur, and how precarious work can be. So I've always kept an eye out for the rainy day. Now this new challenge meant that I would have to forget about that rainy day and invest in the new band. Ken Johnson had no money so I could expect no help from him; I decided to go it alone. Thank goodness, I did manage it. We had a fine band and after about six weeks of hard work at rehearsals I managed to knock them into shape and got a sound somewhat like the then-popular American bands. We started out on the road doing cinema dates; the cinema was then a very popular attraction. And we got a good slick show together. All the boys were in cream evening dress – with plenty of eyes and teeth adding to the display. Ken did his stair dance and fronted the band, and Winnie Cooper, a local girl with a pleasant contralto voice, sang. We were well received everywhere we went, and as the show got well worked in the boys began to add little bits here and there, until we felt that we were just right. Because we were an unknown group, at first the management put the screws on us financially: we realised that we would have to pay a price if we wanted to get to the top. So we ate humble pie, and got just enough to cover our expenses and have a little pocket money.

After about six months, when we were playing in Sheffield, a London agent named Ralph Deane came around to see us, and he said that with our drawing power we were wasting our time roaming around the country. What we needed was a shop window, a good job in the West End, where interested folk could come and hear and see the band. We agreed with him and said that if he found us the job we would be pleased to come along.

After a couple of months he turned up in Glasgow and showed us a contract for the Old Florida Club in Mayfair's Bruton Mews. We were to commence on New Year's Eve, 1936. We now felt that our sacrifices were not in vain. So we started, with huge success on that first night. During this time we had become closely knit as a group and Ken and I were just like brothers. We had a six-month contract, so we had plenty of time to settle in, and to develop a style of our own, as well as to win a rather select patronage. All was well until one night when we were on the stand, playing. The contract had been running for some months, but I could hardly believe my ears when Ken said to me that he and Ralph had signed a new contract that day.

We had never discussed or made any arrangement about a new contract or renewing the old one. We were actually playing, so I had to wait until we were off the stand before I could ask Ken about his remark. Oddly enough, although Ken meant that bit of information for me alone, it seems that most of the other lads had heard it, too. When the relief band took over from us and we had all adjourned to the bandroom we turned to Ken Johnson and asked him to repeat his statement. When he did questions came from every quarter. The outcome was that the whole band said to Ken, since you signed that contract alone, you can carry on. We will leave as we joined Leslie's band. That night my band came to an end and they all walked out.

For me it was a terrible blow – a terrible shock. I had staked so much on the band. I had almost given myself over to this band completely, in every way. And I had dealt with Ken as a true friend and brother. Now the shock of his deception caused me to pause, and to think, and to ask the question – what now? It was then that the uncertainty of life and human nature revealed itself to me most vividly. And somehow I wanted to know and to find certainty. All my life I had professed faith in God, but somehow I wasn't sure about a lot of things. There were doubts and fears, and questionings, until in the darkness and in the emptiness of it all the answer broke in on me like a great light. God holds the answer and, if we give ourselves wholly to Him in faith, He will supply not only the answer, but all our needs as well, for spirit, soul, and body. As a result of my discovery I responded to that call of God, in my soul, and I began to seek Him in prayer, His word, and in fellowship with His people.

As a result I began to gain the assurance and knowledge with certainty, which up to that point I had lacked. Then, as a result of submitting myself and responding fully to the authority of God's word I began to observe that the most striking characteristic of God's people and believers was the element of absolute certainty which they all had. They knew – they didn't hope, or wish, or think. They knew. They knew the measure of God's will for their lives, as revealed in God's word, the Holy Bible, and through faith in Him. And this I also found.

They knew that their sins were forgiven. They knew they had eternal life. They knew – beyond all doubt – that if they died this instant, they would be on the way to heaven. Hence the most startling words of scripture – we know. And what did they know? Answer – we know that we have passed from death to life. We know – that we are of God. We know – in Whom we have redemption through His blood, the forgiveness of sins. We know – that to be absent from the body is to be present with the Lord. We know – that nothing can separate us from the love of God, which is in Christ Jesus our Lord.

For by Him we know that we do know. My experience with Ken Johnson brought me to that place of real and living assurance of God's loving kindness. Before I close this chapter I would like you to ask yourself just a simple question. Suppose your life had to end now, what would be your certainty? I found mine, and you can find yours, too, for our needs are all the same. And the good Lord is ever present to receive us, when we obey the call and respond. The end of that encounter with Ken was that he eventually got his own band but, soon after that night when he and his band came to their tragic end, the same stick of bombs that did it only rocked the nearby establishment where I was working. When I reflect I am grateful for the lessons of that encounter, which eventually caused me to pause and take stock of myself and my relationship to God. It has brought me to the place of absolute certainty and assurance about life, for I now know Whom I have believed and am fully persuaded about the future and all that it entails.

NOTES

Chapter One   JAMAICA

1. Charles E. Moody's Union drugstore was burnt out in 1907 and relocated from Orange Street to West Parade.

2. Marcus Garvey (1887–1940) led the largest black mass movement in America from 1919. It was challenged by communists, black reactionaries, and the most powerful governments in the world but its ideas had and still have a huge impact amongst people. His Universal Negro Improvement Association (UNIA) had branches in most states in the USA, the West Indies, Canada, Britain, Australia, Panama, South Africa, Brazil, Nicaragua and elsewhere. Garvey's attempts to emancipate African peoples suggest that he was the most important person in the first half of the twentieth century.

3. Nancy stories or Anancy stories are folk tales found in much of the English-speaking Caribbean. The name comes from the spider hero who appears in most of them, and is not from 'nasty story' or 'nonsense story'. The spider hero is found in West Africa, in the Twi ananse tales of Ghana, for example. The spider hero is a trickster, surviving in a world of large things, very much like Joel Chandler Harris' 'Brer Rabbit' tales. Nancy stories are not only for children, for the spider is cunning in all matters including sex.

4. Alpha Cottage School was started by Miss Justina 'Jessie' Ripoll on 1 May 1880; she later took the religious name of Mother Mary Peter Claver. With two women friends, active in social work in Kingston, she purchased a forty-three acre site on South Camp Road. It had deep gullies in it and was of little value for farming, hence its low price. The site contained a five-roomed cottage 'Alpha Cottage' which gave its name to the enterprise. The Irish Sisters of Mercy, from a base in south London's Bermondsey, sent eight women to aid the

three Jamaicans in December 1890 and in February 1891 the three joined that order. A convent building was followed by a boys' school (with nine pupils) and one for girls. Agriculture, basket-making, needlework, and similar tasks paid for the daily expenses: the school won a gold medal at the 1891 Jamaican exhibition, and that exhibition's art gallery building became the school chapel: it survived the earthquake. Music was part of the school from the 1890s: it was registered as an industrial school and had a small contribution from the government. A printing section was added in 1895; an infant school in the same year; a two-storied elementary school in 1897. Its work spread throughout Jamaica and its anniversary in 1980 attracted much attention.

5.   Born Robert Morgan in Jamaica in the 1860s, Father Rapael travelled to England and America before studying in Sierra Leone. He was then a missionary, first in Liberia and then amongst Afro-Americans in the USA. He then came to Britain, studied at St Aidan's College, Birkenhead (Liverpool) and then at King's College, London, and was ordained. He was based in Philadelphia, in the Episcopal church (linked to Britain's Anglican church), but developed his own views of Christianity and so joined the Holy Orthodox Catholic and Apostolic Church of the East. *African Times and Orient Review*, London February–March 1913, p. 253 (includes photograph).

6.   Lionel Ottley (1889–1922) joined the West India Regiment in Sierra Leone in 1910. He was a Boy Scout commissioner in Kingston in 1915 and is regarded as the founder of Scouting in Jamaica. From 1916 he served in France and his linguistic skills kept him in Paris until shortly before his death, which Leslie Thompson remembered as surprisingly early.

7.   15,601 enrolled; 10,180 men left Jamaica, 968 died and 1,772 were invalided home, where several died later.

Chapter Two   PROFESSION: MUSICIAN

1.   The Original Dixieland Jazz Band arrived earlier in 1919. This was a white group, playing for dancing.

2. William James Gordon (1864–1922) was awarded the Victoria Cross for saving his white officer's life in the Gambia in 1892. He was severely wounded. He came to Britain in 1897 for Victoria's jubilee.

3. The British Empire Exhibition of 1924 attracted between 60,000 and 300,000 visitors a day. It was re-opened in 1925 but despite its popular success, encouraged by special postage stamps issued throughout the British empire, it lost a great deal of money. The massive stadium, used for the 1948 Olympic Games, was demolished in 2003 and a new stadium opened on the site in 2007.

4. Copied from the French army, in Victorian times.

5. Leonard Shadwell Blackden joined the West India Regiment in 1885.

Chapter Three   MY FACE IS MY FORTUNE

1. *West India Committee Circular*, 25 July 1929, p 297, shows he arrived on the *Jamaican Planter* on 15 July 1929.

2. Harold Arundel Moody (1882–1947) led the League of Coloured Peoples from 1931 until his death.

3. John Alexander Barbour-James (1867–1954) was born in Guyana, transferred to the colonial Ghana post office in 1902 and retired in 1917. His family's home was in west London's Acton from 1904; lawyer S. S. A. (Alfred) Cambridge stayed there around 1915. From 1918 until 1938 Barbour-James and his wife Edith were involved in affairs in Britain, in the African Progress Union, the Association of Coloured People, the Islanders Club, and as a founder and officer of the League of Coloured Peoples. They left England in 1938, and lived in Barbados and Guyana, where he died.

4. Cod Hill remarked 'We got darker and darker and darker and Leslie got lighter.'

5. Walton's biographer states that the BBC commissioned this in 1930; Thompson is sure that he played this piece by Walton before 1930.

6. James Boucher's grandfather was Africanus Horton, Sierra Leone author, medical doctor, army officer, and African nationalist. Boucher's father was English.

7. Norris Smith was a black American entertainer living in London.

8. Guitarist Joe Deniz agreed with this. [Interview 31 May 1985.]

9. Noble Sissle and James 'Eubie' Blake broke the colour bar in New York musical theatres in 1921 with Shuffle Along. This set the style for song-and-dance shows and brought them and others to Britain, which Sissle loved and returned to many times as a singer and bandleader.

10. Polydor files show this session was on 7 November 1934. [Information from Marc Monneraye.]

11. Pierre de Caillaux, or Lionel Jones, was from Ohio and had been in the Southern Syncopated Orchestra around 1920. In a discussion with Arthur Briggs, who played the trumpet in that group from 1919, he was described as 'a very fine, wonderful musician' who had been in Paris in 1940. Briggs thought he was from Canada. [Interview with Briggs, 6 and 7 January 1983].

12. See Sid Colin, *And the Bands Played On*, pp 59-67.

13. Arthur Briggs suggested that both Nancy Cunard and Henry Crowder were drug users, and expressed a low opinion of Crowder's piano skills, suggesting that he used only three fingers. [Interview, January 1983.]

14. Johnson was born in Guyana in 1914, and studied in Marlow, Buckinghamshire.

15. Sidney Bron Music Publishing, later taken over by EMI.

16. Frank Williams from Trinidad was a trumpeter.

17. A veteran's comment, 'He couldn't tell B-flat from a pig's foot.'

18. Jessie Matthews and Sonnie Hale were leading stage performers of the 1930s who appeared at the London Palladium among other top venues.

19. Grant, born Guiana 1905, played clarinet and saxes; Ford, born

Trinidad c.1890 played guitar and string bass.

20. John Chilton, *Who's Who of British Jazz*, states that Hutchinson suffered fatal injuries in a band bus crash in Norfolk and gives the date of death as 22 November 1959.

Chapter Four   BOMBADIER CELLIST

1. Scarth came out with a new-style trumpet and used Leslie Thompson – showing his position as a leading trumpeter in England at that time – in his promotional advertising of the instrument to the trade.

2. The first landed in London in June 1944.

3. 'Pennsylvania 6-5000' was a massive hit for Glenn Miller's orchestra.

4. Organised by London's Black Cultural Archives centre.

5. *Africa: Britain's Third Empire*, published in late 1949.

Chapter Five   WARDEN

1. Found in people of African descent, being nature's anti-malaria protection, sickle cell remains ill-researched as medicine is largely white-dominated.

Chapter Six   PROBATION AND PRISON

2. Edward R. Braithwaite's book was published in London in 1959.

Chapter Eight   AFRICA AND JAMAICA

1. James Hannington, killed October 1885. Within a year 200 African Christians were killed. Their faith in severe adversity marks the beginning of Uganda's Christian period.

2. Idi Amin, army commander, seized power in 1971 and was overthrown in 1979 by the army of Tanzania, an African intervention in the affairs of another state which perhaps marks a maturity in modern African affairs.

3. Janani Luwum was murdered 17 February 1977. Then numerous states severed their links with Uganda, which might now be seen as the end of a white paternal view of independent Africa.

FURTHER READING

Jamaican music of the 1920s is detailed in Ivy Baxter *Arts of an Island* (1970), Coleridge Goode and Roger Cotterrell *Bass Lines: A Life in Jazz* (2002), and Ethel Marson *George Davis Goode: The Man and His Work* (1964). Brian Dyde *The Empty Sleeve: The Story of the West India Regiments of the British Army* (1997) has photographs of Sgt Gordon, V.C., and the regiment band at Wembley in 1924 but Thompson has been cropped.

John Chilton *Who's Who of British Jazz* 2nd edition (2004) details the careers of Blake, Craig, Deniz, de Souza, Dunbar, Foresythe, Goode, Hutchinson, Johnson, King, Stephenson, Thompson and Wilkins. Some have entries in the *Oxford Dictionary of National Biography* as do Barbour-James and Drs J. J. Brown and Harold Moody.

Spike Hughes *Second Movement* (1951) and Chris Goddard *Jazz Away from Home* (1979) deserve attention although Goddard's photo of Louis Armstrong in Turin in 1934 is actually Leslie Thompson.

Black British Swing: the African Diaspora's Contribution to England's Own Jazz of the 1930s and 1940s on Topic Records CD TSCD781 has a useful booklet by Andrew Simons.

For British high society of the 1930s see Charlotte Breese *Hutch* (1999), Ann Chisholm *Nancy Cunard* (1979), Sid Colin *And the Bands Played On* (1980), Richard Hough *Edwina Countess Mountbatten of Burma* (1983), and Carol Kennedy *Mayfair: A Social History* (1986).

Richard Fawkes *Fighting for a Laugh: Entertaining the British and American Armed Forces 1939–1946* (1978) and Colin Grant *Negro with a Hat: The Rise and Fall of Marcus Garvey and his Dream of Mother Africa* (2008) are useful.

Peter Fryer *Staying Power: The History of Black People in Britain* (1984) remains in print and provides a background. Edward R. Braithwaite *To Sir, with Love* (1959), Joyce Eggington *They Seek a Living* (1957), Donald Hinds *Journey to an Illusion: The West Indian in Britain* (1966),

E. Martin Noble *Jamaica Airman* (1984), and Sheila Patterson *Dark Strangers: A Study of West Indians in London* (1963) describe Caribbean migrant experiences of 1950s Britain. Edward Pilkington *Beyond the Mother Country: West Indians and the Notting Hill White Riots* (1988) and Robert Winder *Bloody Foreigners: the Story of Immigration to Britain* (2004) should not be overlooked.

APPENDIX A

VALUES AND PERSPECTIVES

The Editor asked me to write this article which almost makes me question his sense of values and perspective, but as he happens to be the Editor, I guess he has got a lot of what he has got.

Two days ago, the father of a bright boy asked me a question, which is largely responsible for this waste of space. He wanted his boy to become a musician, and was desirous of knowing the best instrument for him to commence studying.

The question seems simple enough, but there is more in it than catches the eye, for the whole future of that boy depends on the soundness of the answer.

First of all let us get acquainted with our little protégé. Alfred is nine years old, well-built, very intelligent, with a bright, cheerful disposition, and a great love for music and animals. His musical weakness is the trumpet, and Louis Armstrong his hero.

This is all perfectly natural for a child of the post-war generation, but there are bigger angles which the youthful mind of the child cannot comprehend.

Let us now take a look at the merits and demerits of the boy's musical choice.

The trumpet is undoubtedly one of the most fashionable instruments of the day, capable of expressing nearly all the idioms of jazz, possesses a beautiful commanding tone, which makes it the natural lead instrument of the modern dance orchestra, and in the hands of a very capable player will attract a good deal of attention, which naturally increases the player's popularity and commercial value.

On the other hand, this instrument depends largely on the embouchure of the player, which, unfortunately, is only reliable up to the prime of manhood, and it is at all times a very delicate and uncertain vehicle for one's existence. Some players are lucky, but those are the ones whom the gods favour. Alfred may become a great player, and if he is lucky he may be able to retire comfortably as soon as his embouchure begins to deteriorate. But if he is unlucky, what then? I leave that to your imagination.

Perhaps you are wondering what my answer to the question is, so I will tell you: I advised the father to let his boy commence the trumpet, but only on the condition that he studies another instrument in conjunction, which is less precarious – preferably the piano, organ, violin, drums or guitar, for if he is a true musician at heart, he will be better able to give full expression to his feelings always, and ensure a sound grasp of the higher branches of the art.

If showmanship is his forte, then he has unlimited resources without being handicapped by the small, but very vital physical factor, the embouchure. Besides, his ambition will be fully gratified by the trumpet, and if he isn't one of the lucky ones, when the time comes, he will be very grateful for his father's keen foresight.

Reprinted from *Musical News*, October 1935, p 11.

APPENDIX B

OPINIONS

'I was devoted to Leslie; he was a cheerful, smiling companion with a mouthful of brilliant white teeth, a soft, musical voice and great charm of manner.' Spike Hughes, *Second Movement*, p 102

'I didn't know Leslie Thompson personally, though I remember that Spike Hughes spoke well of his abilities and other musicians I knew in the early 30s regarded him as a very useful 'doubling' man. By 1934 I had though got to know Louis [Armstrong] quite well. So when Louis was talking about strengthening his band I mentioned Thompson to him as someone who would improve the brass section . . . . Later no doubt Spike told Benny Carter about him. So did I; I remember getting out a list of likely people for Benny.' Jeff Aldam, London, September 1985

'I have known and loved Leslie Thompson since I was introduced to him in a little musical instrument shop in Charing Cross Road in 1929 by the late George Scarth, the proprietor . . . . Here was a man of great charm and a fine musician and when I further discovered that he could hit high notes on the trumpet with greater ease than Louis – well, the band had to be formed around him . . . . What a staunch friend I had found in Tommy. He helped and supported me in those days of long ago when I was only eighteen and fronting a band of chaps all in their mid-twenties or thirties. In actual fact it was Tommy who advised me to go in for the double bass seriously as he seemed to think I had some sort of flare for it. This was after some sort of late night 'do' for the entertainment world under flood-lights at the Ace of Spades on the old Kingston by-pass with my Riviera Hotel sextet and I went on the bass. Jack Hylton, Percival Mackey, Billy Mason, all came up and told me to come and see them but, being a flautist and saxophone player, I knew I didn't have any real technical knowledge of the bass – playing it more or less by ear – so I refrained from going to see them. I took Leslie's advice and went and had tuition with Eugene Cruft, a principal bass with the BBC Symphony Orchestra. So, whatever success I achieved in later years as a bass player can really be laid at Tommy's feet . . . . Tom still comes once in a while to see me and it is always an event I look forward to for he is as full of fun as ever. 'Tom,' I used to say, "When you sunbathe you go a lighter brown and when we whites sunbathe we all try to go brown." Funny, isn't it?' Nigel 'Cod' Hill, Exeter, September 1985

'He was a wonderful first trumpeter – for shows, that sort of thing. That was his line . . . . I admired his technique and his finesse. He had studied and knew exactly what he was doing.' Arthur Briggs, Paris, interview January 1983

'Leslie Thompson was a hell of a nice guy. He didn't bother too much about the rhythm section – he concentrated on the front line, and our rehearsals were stop, start, stop, start: starting, and restarting, until everything was perfect. Leslie Thompson was – is – a musical perfectionist.' Joe Deniz, London, interview September 1985

'I first met Leslie Thompson in 1954 when as a student I was residing at The Alliance Club, a students' hostel at No 2 Bedford Place, Bloomsbury, run by the World Evangelical Alliance. Leslie, as he was affectionately known to all, old and young, had assumed the responsibilities of Warden. He soon demonstrated the characteristics of a fine Christian gentleman, with a dynamic and charming personality, respected and loved by all who came into contact with him.

Leslie and I became good friends as a result, no doubt, of our common West Indian heritage and our Christian faith. In 1955 he was best man at my wedding and has been a dear friend of the family ever since.' Eustace Cummings, Surrey, October 1985

APPENDIX C

BLINDFOLD TEST

An idea originating in America some years ago was adopted with Leslie Thompson. Jazz musicians have developed styles and individual tones, which can be recognised after careful listening. It became the practice to detail who plays what instrument, but this information can prejudice the listener. A 'blindfold test' avoids that prejudice, and clears the mind, so shortly after his eighty-fourth birthday a number of records were played to Leslie, without any details in advance – as if he had been blindfolded: so he had only his ears to guide him.

Reginald Foresythe and Orchestra, 1936
'Mead and Woad'
Is that Briggs? Good English rhythm music. Definitely one of those studio affairs, where good men were brought into the studio and governed by paper. A lot of reading to be done. This kept them to a strict orthodoxy as they were improvising. You can hear from the piano solo that it was Reggie.

Ken Johnson and his West Indian Orchestra, 1938
'Snakehips Swing'
The tenor sounds like Buddy Featherstonaugh. Good ensemble writing.

Ken 'Snakehips' Johnson and his West Indian Orchestra, 1940
'Tuxedo Junction'
Either Tommy McQuater or Dave Wilkins. That's the standard we started out on. Ken had it to jump on, and to carry through. That could have been Leslie Hutchinson, he was a leading black musician by then.

Cyril Blake and his Jig's Club Band, 1941
'Cyril's Blues'

That's real jazz – so different and un-English. Those boys play a different kind of swing to the Americans. A mixture of the West Indies, as opposed to down South, even in the players themselves. That was influenced by the early records of Armstrong's groups – everybody having a go.

Harry Parry and his Radio Rhythm Club Orchestra, 1942
'I Can't Dance'

One of Ken's famous old numbers. That's either Barriteau or Parry. A pity about that boy: a great clarinet player. Thirty years ago I would have been able to give you their names: this is probably Wilkins. His lip doesn't allow him to be daring – he plays within a certain range.

Harry Parry and his Radio Rhythm Club Orchestra, 1942
'Crazy Rhythm'

Who is the guitarist? [Lauderic Caton]. Who is that vibes player? – I can see him now. I can't think of his name. Very good performances.

Billy Merrin and his Commanders, 1936
'Organ Grinder's Swing'

[That's your trumpet solo]. Well, I didn't recognise myself there.

Sam Manning, 1928
'Lieutenant Julian'

I haven't the faintest idea who, where, what, why or when. [It was Sam Manning]. It must be at least sixty years ago since I heard Manning sing. The words are good entertainment. Typically West Indian beat – more than American.

Arizona Dranes, 1928
'He Is My Story'

You can tell it was quite young, in recording, for the voices that should have been near the microphone were distant: you can hardly hear the violin player. The tone was lost. The recorder didn't place the people properly. As far as the West Indies are concerned, religion has been the background of the people. Placed in such a helpless situation as slaves, the only hope a man had was to have a faith. Movement of materialism has touched down in those islands, but the people themselves have not lost that sense of religion. In the early years they believed and practised it; today they don't practise it. Mahalia Jackson – it was so real to her, that she would sing about her Lord to a concert hall full of people and touch them all – an instance of the souls of the people being kept alive. Commercialism, now and then, has recorded some good gospel music.

Benny Carter and his Orchestra, 1936
'Accent on Swing'

Stock arrangement, this is. Is this one of Spike's records? These players sound like players I know, but I wouldn't be sure. Well practised sax section, that – absolutely perfect.

Spike Hughes and his All American Orchestra, 1933
'Sweet Sue, Just You'

Sounds like Tommy McQuater all right. Is it an American record? [Yes], I know that playing. Now that sounds like Benny Carter. Was it Higginbotham, trombone? [No – Dicky Wells]. You couldn't mistake Carter in this. What's that trumpeter's name, now? [Red Allen]. I don't think that was Coleman Hawkins – no, Chu Berry. I never met Wayman Carver but I always admired his playing. He put the flute in jazz.

Mills Brothers, mid-1930s
'Swing Is the Thing'

Marvellous, marvellous. A wonderful group, that. Never had a repetition of them: that group stood for all time. The Mills Brothers. And the Boswell Sisters – another group that hasn't been reproduced. The bass voice – the original fellow – was so deep and penetrating that you would think it was a string bass. I loved the trumpet – the chap who imitated a trumpet. He has wonderful style. I haven't heard this sort of thing since – when I was a teacher for the L.C.C. (London County Council). I was a specialist teacher, for in the late 1940s they didn't have music teachers in schools and multi-instrumentalists were selected and we went from one school to another – the Wren, Oratory, and so on. So I never had time to listen to records after the war, the end of the war. At work, when the other band was playing, sometimes one of the chaps would bring out the odd record and say 'Listen to this,' but I last heard the Mills Brothers in – must be 1940.

Jack Celestain and his Caribbean Stompers, 1928
'Nancy'

Was this recorded in Trinidad? [No – New York, by Trinidadians]. They certainly brought the West Indian element into the studio that time. Very West Indian playing – absolute West Indian style – you can't mistake it at all. It would be lovely if that record was made now, with full equipment. If it had a bass, to give it the guts. A real bit of West Indian music, that was.

Louis Armstrong and his Orchestra, 1935
'Thanks a Million'

Did anyone ever miss that player? Oh my goodness – absolutely marvellous. He's playing straight now – the tune. Terrific. You can't say any more – absolutely terrific. At the time he made that record there weren't many trumpet players who could go up to that top note – top F, concert E-flat.

GLOSSARY

Ackee	Jamaican fruit, used in cooking.
Allenby	British General whose forces captured Jerusalem in 1917.
Archer Street	London location of Musicians' Union and thus centre for musicians seeking work.
Armistice Day	Sunday nearest 11 November: the date of cease-fire of 1918.
Atkins, Tommy	Common soldier.
ATS	Auxilary Territorial Service; the women's branch of the British army in World War 2.
Bass broom	Street sweeper's broom of coarse materials.
Belgravia, London.	District around Belgrave Square,
Blue, tennis	Student who has represented a university in sport (tennis).
Boxing Day	26 December.
Carnation milk	Canned milk, rather sweet.
Civvy Street	Military terms describing civilian life.
Crammer, law	Tutor specialising in law training of a concentrated sort.
Cries of London	Short melodic shouts of street vendors, identifying merchandise or service on offer; sometimes collected in music books.
Demob	Discharge from military service; end of conscript's term.
DHSS	British government department responsible for 1980s unemployment payments.
Digs	Accommodation, generally without cooking facilities.
Doodle-bugs	Rocket bombs or V-l.
ENSA	Entertainments National Service Association; organisation to entertain British military personnel.

'Felix Kept On Walking'   Song about pre-Disney cartoon cat named Felix: black with white paws, hence contrasted to West India Regiment band which had white stockings.

Flunkey   Man servant or uniformed commissionaire.

Ganja   Grass, pot, or marijuana.

Gig   Period of employment and/ place of employment for musicians.

Golliwog   Black doll with big eyes and spiky hair, formerly popular with British children; also term of contempt for Black people.

Grace and favour   Charitable action, usually concerning accommodation, in recognition of past service.

Guinea   £1.05: once a coin of that value.

Harley Street   London street, the centre of Britain's medical profession.

Howsa   Minstrel-type entertainment, with much laughing and talk.

Mau Mau   Anti-colonial movement by Kenya Africans in 1950s.

Mayfair   London's most expensive residential area

Meat and two veg   Meal of meat and two vegetables (one usually potatoes) largely expected by Britons as chief meal of the day.

Muggin'   Fooling around; portraying a fool to entertain others.

NAAFI   Military social club and shop.

N.C.O.   Non-commissioned officer: eg. corporal, sergeant, or warrant officer.

Spud bashing   Preparing potatoes (spuds) or other vegetables.

Toscanini   Italian orchestral conductor, much admired in 1930s Britain.

Tuck shop   Candy shop, snack bar.

Americans should convert British pounds at five dollars, until the 1950s when the pound halved in value.

INDEX

1931 Revue, 73-74, 76

Abbey, Leon, 80, 82, 85
Ableton, Horace, 66
Abraham (Biblical), 131
Adelphi Theatre, London, 40,
    65-6, 77-8
Adkins (bandmaster), 151
African Suite, 109
Ahulu, Felix Konotui, 137
Ainslie, Sgt, 22
Alakija, Dele, 61, 154
Alakija, Tunde, 61, 74, 109, 154
Albert Hall, London, 32
Allenby, Edmund, (Genl, later
    Field Marshall), 20
Alliance Club, London, 4, 128-
    31, 134-8, 141, 143, 150, 159,
    162
Alpha School, 12-13, 15-16, 18,
    20, 37, 39, 92, 100-1, 104,
    164-5
Amin, Idi, 130, 162-3
Amore, Reg, 94, 97
Anderson, Tom, 137
Anti-Aircraft regiment, 105-20
Appleton, Joe, 36, 57-8, 61, 64,
    66, 80, 124
Archer Street, 60, 122
Armstrong, Louis, 61, 64,
    69, 71, 79-85, 87, 89,
    101-2, 107, 132-3
Ashton, Frederick, 78
Astaire, Fred, 74

Atkinson (student), 28
ATS, 113, 116, 118-20

Bag O' Nails club, London, 104
Baker, Josephine, 90-1, 100
Balfour, Arthur, 76
Ball, Captain, 111
Barbour-James, John Alexander,
    67
Baretto (pianist), 80
Barnes, Binnie, 76
Barriteau, Carl, 98
Barrow, Errol, 101
BBC, 105
Beale, John, 137
Bechet, Sidney, 65
Beckles, Milton, 26-7, 31, 44
Bedward (religious leader), 13
Beecham, Thomas, 73, 78
Beek, Ernest, 16, 21, 23, 52
Beethoven, Ludwig van, 123
'Begin the Beguine', 123
Bell, Vanessa, 78
Belshazzar's Feast, 73, 78
Bennett, Robert Russell, 77
Berry, Nyas, 90
Beust, Aylmer, 125
Bingham, Frisco, 84, 91
Blackbirds, 82, 85-6, 88, 100
Blackden, Leonard Shadwell, 51
Blake, George 'Happy', 87, 93
Blake, Cyril, 86, 102
Blake, James 'Eubie', 43, 55-6
Bolland, Miss, 118

Boucher, James 'Jim', 75
Bournemouth Baths, Kingston, Jamaica, 19, 41
Bow Street court, 141
Bowen, Wally, 97, 103
Bowlly, Al, 110
Boy Scouts, 13
Bradley, Clarence 'Buddy', 74, 78, 93
Brahms, Johannes, 20
Braithwaite, Miss, 140
'Brazil', 123
Breakspear, Amy, 19, 39
Bricktop (Ada Smith Du Congé), 84
    Bricktop's club, Paris, 84
Briggs, Arthur, 75, 83, 89
Brison, Carl, 64
British Empire Exhibition, Wembley, 43-5, 152
British West Indies Regiment, 21, 24
Bron (music publisher), 94
Brown Birds, 60-1, 91, 100
Brown, Gerald, 65
Brown, James Jackson, 62-5, 67-8
Brown, Leslie, 65-8, 77, 108
Brown, Milly, 63-4
Brown, Willie, 40-1
Brun, Philippe, 85
'Buenos Aires 6-5000', 121
Bundy, Alfred E, 69
Burston, Reginald, 77
Busby, Lad, 101
Busch, Adolf, 73

Cacelard (cornet player), 46
Café de Paris, London, 106, 110

Callender, 'Nimble', 17, 20, 29, 36, 54
Calloway, Cab, 104
Cambridge, Alfred, 63
Cambridge, Lou, 63
Campbell, Granville, 42
Canadian National Exhibition, 38
Canadian Planter (ship), 38
Carey, John, 137
Caroll, Eddie, 96
Carter, Bennett 'Benny', 90, 98-100
Carter, Howard, 55
Caruso, Enrico, 42
Caton, Lauderic, 102
Cavalcade, 68-9, 76-7, 133
Cellier, Frank, 55
China, Jack, 70-1
Chisholm, George, 100, 102
Chittison, Herman, 82
Chopin, Frederic, 20
Church Commissioners, 107-8
Churchill, Sarah, 78
Churchill, Winston, 121
CIA, 166-7
Ciro's club, London, 76, 80, 89-90, 122-3
Clapham, George, 64-6, 82, 92
Clare, Abe 'Pops', 94, 97
Clarke, Cedric Belfield, 131-2
Clerk, Astley (music shop), 53
Clerk, Winnifred, 53
Clunis (clarinettist), 46
Cobb, John, 143-144
Cochran, Charles B., 60, 66, 68, 73-9, 84, 87-8, 93, 100, 105

Coconut Grove, London, 106, 109-10
Coldstream Guards, 29
Coleman, Stanley, 61-2
Coleridge-Taylor, Samuel, 32, 124
Coliseum, London, 85-6
Collins, Johnny, 83
Conroy, Reg, 70
Constantine, Learie, 124, 142-3
Cook, Lady, 68
Cook, Will Marion, 32
Cooper, Winnie, 94, 97, 174
Cork, Sylvester, 36, 44
Cossack club, 122
Coward, Noel, 65, 76-8
Coward, Sgt, 22
Cox, Hugh Erick Harwood, 41
Craig, Alfie, 85
Creatore's band, 38
Criterion Theatre, London, 106
Cross and the Switchblade, 144
Crowder, Henry, 92
Cuba Club, London, 87
Cunard, Nancy, 92
Cupidon, Ernest, 66-7

Da Costa, Altamont, 44
Davies, Lew, 72
Davis, Clifton 'Pike', 85, 88, 92
Davis, Pike, 88
Dawkin, Oscar, 66, 92
De Caillaux, Pierre , 86
De Chantal, Mother, 12-13, 34
De Souza, Yorke, 87, 93-8, 103
Deane, Ralph, 174
Debussy, Claude, 77
Decca, 71, 74, 78, 92, 106

Decca-Dents band, 72
Delgado (bandsman), 36
Delgado, Ruby Marion, 53
Deniz, Frank, 102, 105
Deniz, Joe, 66, 87, 94-7, 102-3, 110
Derbyshire, Joe, 55
Dibbin, Arthur, 62, 94, 97, 103
Dove, Evelyn, 61-2, 68
Dowling, Lieutenant, 118
Drury Lane Theatre, London, 31, 40, 99
Drysdale, Louis, 43, 56, 65, 68, 75-6
Du Congé, Peter, 80, 83-4 (and Ada – see also Bricktop)
Dudley, Bessie, 90
Duffy, Billy, 122
Dunbar, Rudolph, 63, 77, 79, 87, 124
Dyson, Frank, 36, 44

East Yorkshire Regiment, 51
Edward, Prince of Wales, 76-7
Edwards, E. P., 29
Edwards, Elsie, 77
'Eli, Eli', 58
Elizabeth, Queen (and Princess), 90, 122-3, 128
Ellington, Edward 'Duke', 64, 72, 79, 88, 95, 98, 104
Elliott, 'Piggy', 44
Embassy club, London, 122
Emden (ship), 21
Emperors of Jazz, 97-8, 173
Empire (theatres), 67
Empire Windrush (ship), 124
Empress Hall, London, 132-3

ENSA, 120
Evangelical Alliance, 128
Evelyn, Mr, 141
Ewart, Richard, 36, 44-6

Façade (suite of music), 78
Finch-Hill, Nigel, 70
Follow the Sun, 78-9
Forbes, Vernon, 4
Forde (bandsman), 36, 44
Forde, Brylo, 102
Foresythe, Reginald, 107
Foster, Miss, 125-6
Francis, Harry, 84
Freemasons, 49
Friendship House, Brighton, 137

Gardner, Freddy, 100
Garland, Will, 60-1, 91, 94,
    100, 107
Garrel, Leslie, 36
Garvey, Amy Ashwood, 99
Garvey, Marcus, 10, 35, 37, 55,
    99
Geary, Owen W, 151-2
George V, King, 107
George VI, King, 107
Gilbert and Sullivan, 18
Gladwell, Graham, 137
Gleaner newspaper, 4, 24, 43,
    65
Goddard, Sgt, 92
Goode, George Davis, 23-4,
    39, 73, 78
Goossens, Sidonie, 73
Gordon, William James, 37-8,
    54
Gounod, Charles, 30
Grant, Freddy, 101-2

Gravesande, Sgt, 52
Green Howards regiment, 41,
    51
Greenbaum, Ronnie ('Bumps'),
    73, 77-8
Greenslade, Freddie, 94, 97
Grendon Underwood prison,
    155-7
Guildhall School of Music,
    123-5

Halein, Sonnie, 100
Hall, Adelaide, 109
Hall, Henry, 90
Halsey, Captain, 96
Hamilton, Jack, 82
Handel, George Frederick, 165
Hannington, Bishop, 161
Harling, Cyril, 70, 121
Harrison, 'Captain', 75
Hatch, Ike, 75, 86
Hawkins, Coleman, 85, 96, 100
Haydn, Franz Joseph, 123
Hayes, Harry, 100
Heath, Ted, 124
Hebrew Melodies (sheet music),
    58
Henderson (bandsman), 36
Heywood (bandsman), 36
Hiawatha (cantata), 32
High Yellow (ballet), 78
Hill, Nigel 'Cod', 68-71, 75, 79,
    91
His Majesty's Theatre, London,
    40, 77
'Holy City', 151
Holy Trinity Cathedral,
    Kingston, 13, 23
Howie, Jock, 41, 51

Hudson (organist), 112-3
Hughes, Mrs, 153
Hughes, Spike, 71-3, 76-7, 96, 100
Hunter, Alberta, 90
Hutchinson family, 11
Hutchinson, Leslie 'Hutch', 76, 86, 89
Hutchinson, Leslie 'Jiver', 36, 44, 92-4, 97-8, 103, 110
Hylton, Jack, 85

'I Got a Robe', 62
I Pagliacci (opera), 75
Inglez, Roberto, 103, 105
Institute of Education, London, 130
Isow, Jack, 86

Jacob (Biblical), 44, 131
Jamaica Military Band, 47, 165
Jamaican High Commission, 159
Jamaican Mutual Life Assurance Company, 108
Jamaican Philharmonic Symphony Orchestra, 24
Jamaicans With Backbone, 52
James, Eddie, 143-5
Jemmott, Lily, 61, 64, 66
Jennings, Gerald 'Al', 63-6, 68, 82, 92
Jig's club, London, 68, 88, 90, 102, 104
Johnson, Charlie, 80, 82, 84
Johnson, Ken 'Snakehips', 93-4, 96-8, 102, 104, 106-7, 109-10, 172-6
West Indian Swing Band, 98
Jones (bandmaster), 151

Joseph (Biblical), 1, 16, 131, 140
Joyce, Teddy, 96

Kern, Jerome, 77
King's Regulations, 35
King, Bertie, 92, 94, 96-7, 100, 103, 106
Kirkaldy, Peter, 55
Kitchin, Sam, 24
Kivengere, Festo, 130, 162
Kneller Hall, Twickenham, 16-17, 20, 23, 27-35, 45-6, 52, 54, 76-7, 113, 151
Kneller, Sir Godfrey, 28
Knibbs, 'Fitz', 36, 44
Knibbs, Arthur, 44
Knibbs, Sgt Uriah, 37, 52

Lambe (tutor), 29
Lambert, Constant, 73
Lamont, Edna, 52
Lawrence, Marie, 43
League of Coloured Peoples, 132
Leahong, Thomas, 8-9
Lecesne, Oscar, 15
Leekam, Felix 'Harry', 65
Leekam, Ferdinand 'Ferdie', 65
Leggett (tutor), 29
Lever, Warrant Officer, 22
Lewis, John Richard 'Jacky', 19, 39-41, 52, 77
Linstead Market, Jamaica, 7
Lloyd Jones, Martin, 155
London Bible College, 4
London Hospital, 65
London Symphony Orchestra, 78
London, Edward 'Jack', 67-9, 76, 133

Longman's Music Course, 15, 29
Lopez, Ramon, 122
Lucia di Lammermoor (opera), 38
Lunceford, Jimmie, 64, 95
Luwum, Archbishop Janant, 162
Lyceum Theatre, London, 31
Lyon, John Henry, 154, 156
Lyons Corner Houses, 43

Macfarlane (variety agent), 101
Mackey, Percival, 74
Madden, Cecil, 105
Maida Vale studios, London, 100
Manley, Vera, 23-4, 52-3, 123
Manning, Sam, 56, 90, 99
Markova, Alicia, 78
Marks (student), 31
Martini's Restaurant, 110
Marum, Kitty, 116-7, 149
Mason, Billy, 79
Matthews, Jessie, 100
Maxwell, Clinton, 101-2
Mayfair Hotel, London, 105
McBain (bandsman), 151
McClean, Arthur, 26-7, 31, 36
McClean, Willie, 36
McClean,'Chappie', 36, 45
McCord, Castor 'Cass', 82-5, 88
McMorris, Basil, 4
McQuater, Tommy, 100
Melachrino, Sgt Maj
    George, 120
Melford, Jack, 70
Melody Maker, 124
'Memories Of You', 71
Mendez, Trini, 68
Merrin, Billy, 91

Meyrick, Kate, 92
Mico School, Kingston,
    Jamaica, 2
'Mighty Lak a Rose', 62
Miller, Glenn, 88, 120
Mills Brothers, 102
Mills, Florence, 43, 65
Milton, Mr, 141
Mireille, 30
Misso, Dudley, 103, 105
Monolulu, Prince, 109
Moody, Harold, 5, 67-8, 130
Moody, Ludlow, 23, 52-53
Moody, Vera, 23, 53, 56
Mountbatten, Countess, 90
Movies theatre, Cross Roads,
    Jamaica, 20, 39-41, 49, 55
Mozart, Wolfgang Amadeus,
    123
Mumford-Taylor, Robert, 87,
    94, 97, 102-3, 122
Munro College, Jamaica, 3-4
Murphy, Jacob 'Spud', 36, 44
Music in the Air, 77
Musical Times, 78
Musicians' Union, 84-85, 109
Muzikant and family, 58-9
'My Face Is My Fortune', 71
Myrtle Beach Hotel, Jamaica,
    41

NAAFI, 112, 114-6
Nash, 'Paddy', 36, 38-39, 46
Nation, Henry 'Harry', 23-4
Negro World, 35
Nehru, Jawaharial, 90
Neilson, Sgt George, 36, 44,
    52

Nest Club, London, 68, 85, 88, 90, 100-2, 104
Newton, Isaac Augustus 'Gus', 64, 80
'Nightingale Sang . . . ', 86
Nkrumah, Kwame, 131
Northumberland Rooms, London, 67

O'Connor (bandsman), 26, 31
Oddfellows, 49
Old Florida Club, London, 96, 98, 106-7, 174
Olympic Games, 68
Ottley, Lionel, 16, 45
Owen, Stanley, 29, 34, 38

'Pack Up Your Troubles . . . ', 18
Padmore, George, 126-7
Palace Theatre, Kingston, 39-41, 51, 54-6
Palladium, London, 79, 100
Palmer, Leyland, 13, 15
Parlophone, 79
Payne, John, 68, 76, 90
Pearce, Billy, 74
Pentonville prison, 143, 145-8, 155, 157, 159
Pfister, Father, 18
Philharmonic Hall, London, 32
Phillips, Sid, 101
Phillips, Woolf, 101
Pinafore, 18
Porteus (bandsman), 36
Portman Rooms, London, 58
Pratt, Alfred, 83
Purcell, Patrick Ambrose 'Paddy', 151

Queen Mary (ship), 76

RAF symphony orchestra, 121
Rainey, Jock, 28
Rainford, Roland, 36, 44
Rapael, Father, 13
Reid, Benjamin De Cordova, 37, 52
Rhythm Clubs, 88
Ricketts, Edmund, 20, 35-6, 44, 54
Rimbault's Catechism of Music, 15
Rio Grande (ballet), 73
Roberts, George, 98, 110
Robeson, Paul, 68, 75, 90, 92, 99-100
Rodgers, Gene, 90
Ros, Edmundo, 102-3, 105-7, 109-10, 112, 115, 122
Rose Marie, 31
Rowe, Oscar, 126-7, 150, 154
Royal Academy of Music, 22, 39, 73, 152
Royal Artillery regiment, 107, 113, 117, 120, 124, 151
Royal College of Music, 22
Royal College of Organists, 109
Royal Engineers regiment, 151
Royal Mail Steam Packet Co, 11
Royal Scots regiment, 28
Russell, Ralph, 57

Salome, 73
Savoy Theatre, London, 78
Scarth, George, 69, 107
Scott, Alf, 20, 54, 56, 95
Scott, family, 54, 56
Seaman (student), 27

'Serenade for a Wealthy . . . ', 107
Seventh Dragoons, 32
Shim Sham Club, London, 86, 88
Show Boat, 75
Sims, Stephen, 159-63
'Sirocco', 72, 78
Sissle, Noble, 43, 55, 76-7, 89
Six Bells, 72
'Six Bells Stampede', 72
Skinner, Raymond and Norman, 137
Skipp, Sergeant, 116
Slaughter, Bill, 30
'Slide Mongoose', 18
Smith, Joe 'Manny', 80
Smith, Norris, 75, 86, 90
Snow, Valaida, 90
South, Eddie, 74
Southern Syncopated Orchestra, 32, 46, 68, 83
Sowande, Fela, 109
Spencer (bandsman), 36
St George's College, Jamaica, 3, 18
'St Louis Blues', 81
Stars in Battledress, 3, 120-1
Steinway Hall, London, 65
Stephenson, Louis, 36, 87, 92, 94, 97, 103
Stewart, Eldon, 46, 52
Stewart, Oswald, 36, 44
Straumann (German sailor), 22
Summers, Micky, 62
Sun Never Sets, 99
Swift, George, 85
'Swing Low', 62

Tagg's Island, 69-70, 121
Tatum, Art, 90
Tchaikovsky, Pyotr Ilyich, 123
Thames, Earl, 4
Thomas, Norman, 89
Thompson, Anthony Christopher 'Tony' (son), 116, 149-58
Thompson, Charlotte (mother), 1-2, 8, 12-15, 168
Thompson, Egbert, 32, 45-6, 55-6, 86
Thompson, Emmanuel (father), 1-2, 8, 12-13
Thompson, Maria (sister), 1, 168
Thompson, Mrs (wife), 87, 108, 133, 149-50
Thompson, Wington, 20, 43, 56, 80
Three Choirs Festival, Worcester, 24
'Tiger Rag', 81
Titanic (ship), 4, 12
Turner, Thomas 'Crutch', 44, 46
Tutenkhamen, 55
'Twentieth Century Blues', 76
Tyree, Harry, 64, 82, 86
Tyree, Monty, 64, 66

Union Jack Club, London, 32
Universal Negro Improvement Association, 35, 99
University Challenge (TV / radio programme), 156
Up Park Camp, Jamaica, 9, 22, 30, 36, 50, 165

Vanderpoye, Bruce, 87, 95, 98, 103
Verity, James 'Jim', 39, 77
Verity, Mrs S. J., 39-41

Wallace, Arthur Thompson, 80
Waller, Thomas 'Fats', 90, 100-4,
Walters, Adrian, 36
Walton, Dennis, 102-3, 105-6
Walton, William, 73, 78
Wandsworth prison, 145, 155
Ward Theatre, Kingston, 17, 47-8, 55, 67, 78, 99, 154
Ward, Colonel, 13
Welch, Elisabeth, 100
West End Blues, 71
West India Regiment, 16, 21, 36-9, 44, 47, 51, 80, 94, 140, 164
West Side Story, 144
Westminster Chapel, 155
Weston, Alan, 36
Weston, Harry, 70
Whitborne, Ken, 4
Wilkerson, Reverend David, 144
Wilkins, David Livingstone, 98, 102, 110, 124
Williams (uncle of Jack London), 67-8
Williams, David 'Baba' 98, 110
Williams, Father, 13
Williams, Frank, 95, 115
Williams, Spencer, 90, 101, 107
Wilson, Edith, 90

Wilson, Garland, 90, 104
Wilson, Tom, 94-5, 97, 103
Wiltshire Regiment, 113
Winfield, George, 85, 88, 92
Wolmer's School, Jamaica, 3
Words and Music, 66, 74, 77, 79
Wormwood Scrubs prison, 145

JAZZ BOOKS FROM NORTHWAY

Join our mailing list for details of new books,
events and special offers: write to
Northway Books,
39 Tytherton Road, London N19 4PZ
or email *info@northwaybooks.com*
www.northwaybooks.com

FORTHCOMING JAZZ BOOKS

FROM NORTHWAY

Peter King,
Flying High: A Jazz Life and Beyond

Jim Godbolt,
A History of Jazz in Britain 1919–50 (paperback edition)

JAZZ BOOKS FROM NORTHWAY

Chris Searle,
*Forward Groove: Jazz and the Real World
from Louis Armstrong to Gilad Atzmon.*

Coleridge Goode and Roger Cotterrell,
Bass Lines: A Life in Jazz

Alan Robertson
Joe Harriott – Fire in his Soul

Mike Hennessey,
The Little Giant – The Story of Johnny Griffin

Derek Ansell,
Workout – The Music of Hank Mobley

Digby Fairweather,
Notes from a Jazz Life

Ron Brown with Digby Fairweather,
Nat Gonella – A Life in Jazz

John Chilton,
Hot Jazz, Warm Feet

Graham Collier
the jazz composer – moving music off the paper

Peter Vacher,
Soloists and Sidemen: American Jazz Stories

Jim Godbolt,
A History of Jazz in Britain 1919–50

Jim Godbolt,
All This and Many a Dog

Ronnie Scott with Mike Hennessey,
Some of My Best Friends Are Blues

Vic Ash
I Blew It My Way: Bebop, Big Bands and Sinatra

Ian Carr,
Music Outside

Alan Plater,
Doggin' Around

Harry Gold,
Gold Doubloons and Pieces of Eight

Northway Books,
39 Tytherton Road, London N19 4PZ
info@northwaybooks.com
www.northwaybooks.com